GETTYSBURG AND LEADERSHIP

Principles for Today's Leaders from the Most Terrible Battle Fought in America

James P. Osterhaus

ISBN 978-1-64003-785-4 (Paperback)
ISBN 978-1-64003-786-1 (Digital)

Covenant Books, Inc.
11661 Hwy 707
Murrells Inlet, SC 29576
www.covenantbooks.com

Endorsements

- Excellent read, not only for those particularly interested in the Civil War, but also for those who want to understand the key role good management plays in big issues (war, the economy) and in how we manage the office, family and friendships. I particularly found useful the self-diagnostics at the end of each section. My only complaint, I wish I had had this book in 2003 when I assumed my ambassadorship. The Honorable William Hudson. Former U.S. Ambassador to Tunisa

- Since my commissioning as a Marine officer in 1963, I have had two areas of continuing study and interest: military history and leadership. In *Gettysburg and Leadership,* Jim Osterhaus masterfully extracts effective leadership principles from his insightful analysis of the most significant battle of the Civil War. Not just a great read, but a book to study, absorb, and apply!
Jeff Oster, Lieutenant General, U.S. Marine Corps (Retired)

- Gettysburg and Leadership is a classic. Jim Osterhaus provides the reader with sound leadership principles illustrated by the leadership struggles at the battle of Gettysburg. A book so interesting it is hard to put down. John E. Walker, PhD Founder and Chair of Andesa Services, Inc. Namesake of John E. Walker Dept. of Economics, Clemson University.

- What do you get when you combine a lifetime of counseling and management experience with a love of the lessons of history? The answer is the latest book from Jim Osterhaus, <u>Gettysburg</u>. As Osterhaus demonstrates, leadership is all about facing painful conflict and finding the way through. And as a leader of leaders, he knows the power of historical analogy to help define problems and lead to successful solutions. The Rt. Rev. Neil G. Lebhar, Bishop of the Gulf Atlantic Diocese

- The strategic, transformational and tactical challenges through which Jim has coached me toward becoming a well-defined leader are shared in his latest book Gettysburg and Leadership. Jim draws on the parallel passions of his life – coaching leaders and Civil War history – into a terrific narrative. As this pivotal battle account unfolds, the principles of leadership development necessary to adapt, compete and thrive in a rapidly changing 21st century world also emerge. A compelling read!! Ron Scheese. CEO. Andesa Services Inc.

- This book is terrific and I know I will cite it in upcoming leadership discussions with clients. Rip Tilden. Partner, Makarios Consulting

Acknowledgments

It is impossible to pinpoint all of the influences on me that have gone into crafting this book. I became interested in the Civil War when I was seven years old. Growing up in Northern Virginia near the battlefields, I had easy access to the sites where the battles were fought. My family fought on both sides of the struggle. My great grandfather, in southern cavalry, was captured at Fishers Hill in 1864 and nearly died at Point Lookout before signing Lincoln's oath of allegiance so he could return to Fairfax, Virginia, in early 1865. There he hid in his parents' barn for four months, fearing Mosby's Partisan Rangers. My great uncle, Peter Osterhaus, rose to major general and for a time led a corps under Sherman.

As the years went by, I read pretty much all I could get my hands on, focusing primarily on the people who fought the war. I cannot think of any other time in history where so many odd and interesting characters populated a particular period.

If the reader is interested in further reading into the battle of Gettysburg, there are a number of fine volumes, including eye witness accounts from soldiers and civilians living in Gettysburg. But my favorite volume is Allen Guelzo's *Gettysburg, the Last Invasion*.

I would also recommend reading into the life of Abraham Lincoln. There are many fine volumes out there. Several of my favorites include Allen Guelzo's (yes, he is an excellent writer who is also well researched) *Abraham Lincoln: Redeemer President* and Ronald White's *A. Lincoln*. Guelzo also has a wonderful overview of the war in *Fateful Lightning*.

In relation to all things leadership, there are several people to whom I am indeed indebted, several I've met, others I haven't. If you are familiar with their writings, you will see them pop up over and over in these pages. They include:

Ron Heifetz's understanding of leadership (along with his colleague Marty Linsky) has shaped much of my thinking. Though he has authored and co-authored a number of books, I would highly recommend *The Practice of Adaptive Leadership*.

Jim Collins' work has also been very influential. He came and spoke to a forum my company TAG Consulting held out near his home on Colorado. He is an excellent speaker and writer, and his book *Good to Great* is a must.

Then there's Rabbi Edwin Friedman, now deceased, whose book *Failure of Nerve* is a must for understanding the well-defined leader.

Patrick Lencioni is someone I have not met, but his thinking very much parallels my own. You will see his ideas sprinkled throughout.

I apologize to all the above and possibly more when I have not cited your work as carefully as I could have. Thinking over the years becomes blended, and knowing the demarcation between my own and that of others becomes increasingly difficult.

I also say thank you to all of the folks at TAG Consulting. These people are not just colleagues, but friends and "family." I especially wish to thank Joe Jurkowski, my friend and colleague for some forty years, where he and I have labored in a number of settings together and his mind still tends to astound me; also Kevin Ford, whom I've known for nearly thirty years, in which he and I have also written a couple of books, the most recent being *Secret Sauce*, which more fully explains code and culture and how it is shaped and changed; Ken Tucker, another of my business partners who, along with Kevin, wrote *Leadership Triangle*, which is an amplified discussion on the leadership triangle chapter herein; and then Kurt, Shane, Rich, John, Chris, Bob, Kelly, Ann, Mariana, and a whole host of others who have worked in TAG.

Lastly, I'd like to thank my wife of nearly fifty years, Marcy, who has been my constant companion on the journey.

Introduction

Two great armies, numbering 170,000 men, kicked up clouds of dust as they marched through the late June heat, converging on roads that had drawn generations of farmers from across the rolling countryside toward the market town of Gettysburg in south central Pennsylvania.

These had been armies of contrast. The southern army, though poorly equipped, had been ably led and had scored numerous victories in the eastern theater. Its soldiers had full confidence in their commander, Robert E. Lee. The Union army had been bowed, but not broken. In ways they defied reason and believed in themselves. They had a sense of what they could do if they were properly led. They had watched one incompetent commander after another be second-guessed by Washington politicians. They waited patiently for the commander who would emerge to confidently and competently lead them. Their new commander, installed two days before this moment, was a totally unknown quantity.

These two armies were on a collision course with each other and with history. The great battle they would fight would be the stuff of legend.

The Civil War is arguably the pivotal moment in American history. Next to George Washington, Abraham Lincoln is the greatest leader in American history. At the little hamlet in south central Pennsylvania—the greatest leader and the greatest battle to be fought on American soil—where the battle's fulcrum lies, that convergence would be put into words. These were not just any words. They constituted the most elegant explanation ever placed before the American people regarding the nature and destiny of our nation.

The basic DNA of America cannot be understood without grasping the centrality of the Civil War and Abraham Lincoln. We can look at battlefields and talk of tactics and strategy. We can talk about the intriguing leaders who led thousands of civilian-turned soldiers into a maelstrom that no one now can even imagine (Gettysburg incurred ten times the number of causalities as D-Day). However, the Civil War is much more than this. The Civil War defined who we are as a people (this country, made up of separate states, was forged into a single nation). What emerged in the struggle were some of the most prominent and revered leaders this country and the world has ever seen.

Since childhood, I have been fascinated with the Civil War. Growing up in Northern Virginia within an easy drive of countless battlefields helped. Having direct relatives who fought on both sides of the struggle also helped. As I got older, I tended to focus more on the leaders who had led the regiments, brigades, corps, and armies. And finally, I became captivated by Abraham Lincoln, a man for this moment in our history, a man who stepped out of nowhere with none of the apparent leadership characteristics necessary to become arguably the greatest of all of our nation's leaders.

Because Gettysburg is a defining moment in our history, crafted by leaders who, even after 150 years, are household names, the battle is an excellent moment to study leadership. So who is the effective leader? Volumes have been written on this subject, as people have attempted to come to terms with what this very indispensable element comprises. No one volume can ever capture all of the variables that go into effective leadership.

What is now beginning to creep into leadership literature is the absolute necessity of the leader to look internally, to become more self-aware. The art of command is how a commander (1) sees himself [1](also including his entire force), (2) sees the enemy, and (3) sees the terrain. Leaders will use military science to inform them of any one of those three. However, the art form is understanding or intuiting

---

[1] I use the masculine pronoun *him* throughout the book, because the battle itself was primarily a masculine enterprise. But the principles herein apply equally to men and women.

how the three interrelate. In the past, this has been dismissed as so much psychobabble. But what we are now coming to realize is that leaders who lack self-awareness are leaders who have a much higher propensity to guide their organizations into troubled waters, not out of them.

So who is this leader who is able to make a difference? I would argue she/he is:

1. The well-defined leader, the one who:
   a. Builds trust
   b. Understands the organization as a whole
   c. Aligns the organization
   d. Recognizes the three facets of leadership and responds accordingly
   e. Deals effectively with conflict
   f. Brings about change
   g. Manages the people and raises up the next generation of leadership
   h. Leads transformationally

We will consider each of these elements in turn and in fact how the earlier principles lay the foundation for those that follow. We will narrate significant events of the battle, each of the three days serving as a prism through which we will frame the salient leadership issues that emerge.

Part I

The First Day[2]

The first day of battle, July 1, 1863, would witness two great armies stumbling into each other and accidentally initiating the greatest battle ever fought on the American continent, which is arguably one of the signature battles of world history. Places on the battlefield became the stuff of legend: the Peach Orchard, the Wheatfield, Devil's Den, Little Round Top, Cemetery Ridge, and the Angle. The names of those who fought there have become legendary, even mythical: George Meade, Winfield Hancock, Joshua Chamberlain, Pap Greene, James Longstreet, Robert E. Lee, John Bell Hood, J. E. B. Stuart, and, of course, the members of the two opposing armies.

On this particular hot and humid day in July long ago, the landscape and the roads had conspired to draw these two armies into proximity. But once drawn by the landscape to the small market town, snap decisions at critical moments with minimal information by opposing

---

[2] All maps are taken from Wikipedia, the *Battle of Gettysburg*.

commanders at different command levels of each army would determine how this battle would unfold.

This day, and the following two days, would demand leaders who were self-aware, who had built trust with those who followed them, who understood the code of their organizations, and who understood the scope of their authority while exercising leadership in the most effective manner and successfully aligning and realigning their troops. Some leaders, on these three hot July days, would meet and even exceed expectations. Others would not.

As with militaries engaged in great conflicts, organizational life has a way of either presenting unexpected opportunities or offering unanticipated threats. Successful organizations are able to face these situations, come to terms with the hard realities that unfold, and make the adjustments necessary to move forward.

On this first day of battle, we will consider how leaders must be well defined as individuals and self-aware as people. Once leaders are well defined, they will be able to build trust with those who follow. And having built trust, these leaders will then need to grasp the unique code of their organizations in order to move them forward toward their desired future.

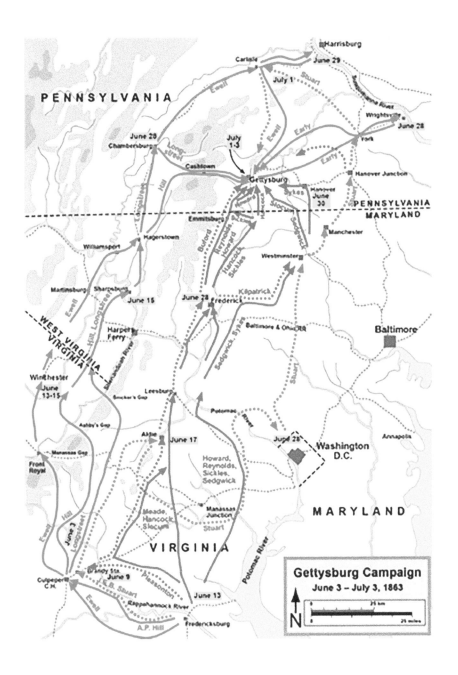

Chapter 1

Who is this person who can best lead our organization to its desired future?

Most everyone would agree that leadership is a critical factor in the functioning of any organization—a family, a club, a faith community, a multinational corporation, or a nation. People have often speculated as to the essential characteristics that make up the effective leader.

The Battle

As the sun began to rise on the muggy morning of July 1, both Lee and Meade, at the head of their respective armies, had no intention of bringing on a major engagement until several issues were plain to both: Where should this battle be fought? What was the strength of the opposing force, and where were the various elements of that force located? What would be the most advantageous location for this fight, and what were the characteristics of the terrain in that area?

Both commanders knew there would be a momentous fight, and to an extent, both would welcome it, but not now and not necessarily here. The above questions still dangled in both generals' minds.

Lee was closer than his adversary to the town of Gettysburg that morning, though he was still some miles west of the town. But he was close enough to hear the firing when it first commenced in the east. Meade was many miles south, still in Maryland, and would have to rely on couriers to inform him that parts of his army were beginning to engage the enemy just outside Gettysburg. He would have to make decisions quickly as to what to do: Engage? Withdraw? Uncertainty gripped both commanders, and this unfolding day would demand quick decisions on each generals' part.

Robert E. Lee

Lee, fifty-seven years of age and considered one of the most dignified and handsome men of his day, had assumed command of the Army of Northern Virginia the previous year, when the Union army was at the gates of Richmond. In appearance and demeanor, he was every inch the soldier and consummate leader.[3]

Unlike his predecessor Joe Johnston, Lee had the full confidence of Confederate President Davis, for whom Lee was military advisor before taking command. Interestingly though, Lee had never been in command. Until he became commander of the Army of Northern Virginia, the only troops he had personally commanded in combat were US Marines storming the fire engine house at Harpers Ferry to capture John Brown and his men in 1859. That battle lasted but minutes.

On the Peninsula the year before, the newly appointed army commander Lee had organized his units and ruthlessly attacked the Union forces. His commanders were unfamiliar with his style. The attacks were uncoordinated and sloppy. But these attacks did the one necessary thing: they sowed fear and doubt in the mind of the Union commander, George B. McClellan.

At first, Lee's own men and the southern public were skeptical about his ability to lead. He was seen as a cautious old man in an age and a

---

3   Lee, at the outset of the war, had been tapped by the army chief of staff and President Lincoln to head the armies of the north. He had rejected the offer and chosen to go with his home state, Virginia, thus becoming quite possibly the only general in history ever to be offered the command of both armies that would face one another.

region that demands bold offensives. But after he took command and launched slashing attack after slashing attack on the Union army confronting him, his critics were silenced.

In three short months, Lee had carried the war from the gates of Richmond to the suburbs of Washington and then into enemy territory. His fellow citizens hailed him as a hero. His men would follow him anywhere. He had begun to believe his men were invincible.

This year of 1862, as Lee's army had entered Maryland for his first invasion, Lee had declared the army was there to help Maryland throw off the yoke of bondage Union occupation had created and restore her citizens to their rights. He hoped the young men of the state would rally to his cause and fill his depleted ranks. Instead, hardly anyone cared, and few responded.

Future generations will question Lee's strategic focus—he had nowhere near the grasp of the entire war unfolding throughout the country as did U.S. Grant—but few can question his tactical abilities. On a battlefield, he was audacity personified, constantly seeking to seize the initiative. His principal strengths lay in his ability to make quick decisions in the face of the enemy, his ability to exploit his opponent's mistakes, and the efficient handling of the forces that were available to him.

His primary failings sprang from his breeding as a southern gentleman in a leading family of Virginia: he was excessively sensitive to the feelings of subordinates and exhibited a repeated reluctance to insist upon his own judgment when contradicted by his underlings. The one place where this latter trait was not in evidence was at Gettysburg (Lee repeatedly refused Longstreet's entreaties), which would prove his undoing.

Tactical theory of the time had been reinforced by tactical experiences on the battlefields of the Mexican War emphasizing the offensive over the defensive, that aggressive flanking assaults could overtake the most entrenched positions. Close order formations allowed commanders to control troops more readily and concentrate fire more effectively. And of course, the bayonet (along with the smoothbore Napoleon cannon which was used when infantry drew close to the enemy) was the darling of the offensive-minded leader. These ideas were well suited to Lee's personality and to the southern mindset generally.

Nearly a year had passed since that first unsuccessful invasion of the North that ended in a bloodbath on the banks of Antietam Creek near Sharpsburg in Maryland. As he moved through Cashtown in south central Pennsylvania, heading down the dusty road toward the rumbles of cannon he was hearing off toward Gettysburg, Lee was full of confidence. He had watched his men repeatedly chase men in blue from battlefield after battlefield. These men could do the impossible. But on this morning of July 1, Lee was unsure as to why he was hearing concentrated cannon fire off to the east. He had expressly commanded that a general engagement not be initiated until the army was concentrated and suitable ground had been selected. What did these ominous sounds portend?

George Gordon Meade

In contrast to Lee, George Meade looks nothing like a soldier, much less the commander of the largest army ever assembled on the American continent. He was forty-seven when the command of the Army was dumped into his lap in June of 1863. When he was aroused from sleep, he thought he was being put under arrest for insubordination to the previous commander, Joe Hooker. Instead, he was handed the army command. He had never wanted to be a soldier in the first place, much less be in charge of the army when it faced its most perilous challenge. Other more qualified generals had turned down the job, knowing that Washington's meddling had brought down each successive general in turn.

Meade displayed nothing of the dazzle of Lee's bearing—though tall, he was a slight man with stooped shoulders, a face dominated by sunken eyes sitting atop a large Roman nose and framed in thinning hair and graying whiskers. On horseback too, he gave the appearance of a grim helmeted knight. He cared little for the pomp of high command. His disposition was explosive, cantankerous, and generally bad-tempered, quite possibly dyspeptic—"a damned old goggle-eyed snapping turtle."

Meade had headed to West Point as the one possibility for obtaining a decent free education, his merchant father having died prematurely following bad investments. His strategy had been to graduate and, after putting in the required time in the army, spring into private life. His plan had worked perfectly, and after fighting Seminole Indians in Florida, he had become a civil engineer. But his civilian career had been rocky, and he took the unusual step of reentering the army as a second lieutenant in the Corps of Engineers. He was a staff officer in the Mexican War, serving with not much distinction. He was a captain who had principally surveyed the Great Lakes and seen the construction of a few lighthouses when the Civil War broke out, and he was summoned by George McClellan to command a Pennsylvania Reserve Division as a brigadier general of volunteers. Meade hoped, as had McClellan, that the war would be limited to reunion and that the cooler moderate heads in the land would prevail.

He performed well on the Peninsula and at Antietam. He then led what became the only near-successful Union attack at Fredericksburg and was promoted to command the V Corps until he was awakened in his tent at four that late June morning in 1863 by a messenger from General Halleck, handing him the army.

When he took over the army, Meade was one of seven corps commanders; and as he took command, he had no idea where the other six corps were located. When he found out, he was shocked that the army was apparently scattered across the landscape. As a general, he had not been great, but he was sound and efficient. Meade was competent, handling troops well, a decent tactician mingled with courage in a crisis. But he lacked the boldness and originality to be seen as a proficient strategist.

He was cautious with good reason. He was now the fourth general to be in charge of this army in less than a year. His appointment did not set off spontaneous paroxysms of joy—most hardly knew who he was. He knew that if he were able to defeat Lee and drive him back south, he would receive little praise; and if he were defeated, he'd be pilloried. The best hand he could play was a safe hand—the hand he had watched his mentor George McClellan play. He decided his best bet would be to concentrate his army in a safe place, an excellent defensive position at Pipe Creek, fifteen miles above Frederick, Maryland. This would shield Washington, DC, and Baltimore. But as General Reynolds pushed the Union's I, III, and XI Corps up toward Emmitsburg to keep an eye on Lee, Pipe Creek would fade in history, the two armies engaging up north in Gettysburg.

In the back of Meade's mind, he must have known he was immediately responsible for eighty to ninety thousand men. And more than that, he was responsible for the protection of the capital and ultimately the safety of the republic.

These two men, Lee and Meade, were the two principal commanders. But their lieutenants—Longstreet, Hill, Ewell, Reynolds, Howard, Hancock, Sickles, Slocum, Sykes, and Sedgwick—also would need to step up and exercise astute leadership as the farm fields, woodlots, hillocks, and dells around Gettysburg filled with smoke and exploded in chaos. Some would comport themselves magnificently. Others would falter and fail.

Two men, at the front of the two largest armies ever to face one another on the American continent, could not have been more different in their looks, personalities, unique talents, and heritage. And yet each in his own particular way would be successful.

The Central Role of Leadership

Leadership is central and critical to optimum organizational functioning. There is little debate as to whether this is true. But what are the traits that set apart those leaders who leave a lasting mark on their organizations and ultimately on their communities? Discussions of leadership characteristics have blended into discussions of leadership style:

a. Autocratic or authoritative
b. Democratic or participatory
c. Laissez-faire or despotic
d. Toxic or life-giving
e. A whole host of other styles that have been noted down through the years

Leadership books abound, containing many excellent ideas as to how leadership should unfold and who is best to lead. In my coaching and assessment of leaders in many different organizational pursuits, I have come to several conclusions: First, there is no best personality/talent profile for an ideal leader. Second, there are several behaviors of leadership that are essential to success. And these activities (each of which to be described in its own chapter) hinge on one key component—a leader who is well defined as a person (we'll describe this in more detail later). If this is not the case, and the leader is not particularly well defined, all manner of dysfunction within the organization (be it a family, a government agency, a religious institution, or a multinational corporation) will prevail. So let's turn to this first key issue, the well-defined leader, which is in turn built on a person who is self-aware.

The Well-Defined Leader

Who is the leader who is able to lead effectively? This question has been a tantalizing one for centuries. It is what we call the well-defined leader. We know from the work of Jim Collins, a well-known researcher into leadership, that he is a person with two qualities: humility (it's not about me) plus focus (it's about the mission), a combination of character and action.[4] But can we dig deeper than this? Can we peer inside these particularly effective leaders to see what actually makes them tick?

The well-defined leader is internally aligned (what he says is what he does). These leaders are able to separate themselves from the surrounding emotional climate so that they can break through the barriers that are keeping everyone from moving forward effectively. In other words, they have strong personal boundaries and, yet, not so rigid that information can't flow in and out altering their perspective from time to time.

This first principle appears so simple. And yet, it is difficult for anyone to remain internally aligned over the long haul. How we become internally misaligned will be more fully discussed in chapter 8. Sufficient to say, it is the internally competing values that tend to misalign us, as we acknowledge one value (I need to spend a great deal of time with my kids), while another value (I must make a great deal of money to justify my existence) actually holds sway in my life

---

[4]   Jim Collins, *Good to Great*

(it has more emotional power behind it), and I spend very little time with my kids. So how do we normally deal with these internal inconsistencies? We deceive ourselves, telling ourselves that all is well, thus giving ourselves a great deal of emotional satisfaction, at the expense of the truth.

As the leader is able to recognize and correct his/her internal inconsistencies, she/he is able to present a non-anxious presence within the organization. And keep in mind, *presence* is so much more important than any method or technique of leadership a person might employ. As a result of this quality, the well-defined, non-anxious person is able to lead effectively. That's right, non-anxious. It is an interesting term when discussing leadership, is it not?

Most people have little understanding of the role that anxiety plays within personal and organizational life. Just as anxiety can spread through a herd of cows once one cow has become upset, so anxiety can permeate an organization as leadership becomes anxious. Anxiety signals are emitted in unconscious behavioral ways and, once released, can spread from person to person like a virus.

One principal way that my anxiety is aroused and stoked is when I am internally misaligned (what we sometimes call incongruent), unable to resolve competing values and assumptions internally. When the leader is incongruent with the attendant anxiety rising as a result, the consequences are so much greater than for anyone else in an organization. That's because everyone in the organization constantly monitors the leader, assessing how he is doing at any given time. If large amounts of anxiety are detected (and it doesn't take much anxiety to arouse those who are poorly defined as people), "smoke detectors" within individuals begin to activate.

Did you notice the word "alignment" in there? It's there because alignment is critical to leadership success, and I'll tell you why. Those who lead, who are internally aligned with their own values (their actions match their words) and thus are able to align the organization around its values, mission, and vision, are the truly effective leaders. And yet, so few leaders across the organizational world seem to possess this essential quality.

The Self-Aware Leader

The most effective leaders, those who are most well defined and internally aligned, are the leaders who are the most self-aware, simple as that. Oh, you say, I'm not into all of the soft psych stuff. If you aren't aware of yourself, then parts of yourself buried deep in your brain will misalign you, controlling much of your thinking and responding. In other words, you may think that your actions are perfectly aligned with what you say and what you value, but research proves otherwise. In fact, our brains are wired to protect ourselves from the truth of our incongruence. So we stumble through life, misaligned, all the while assuming that all is perfectly well and that everyone celebrates us the way we celebrate ourselves.

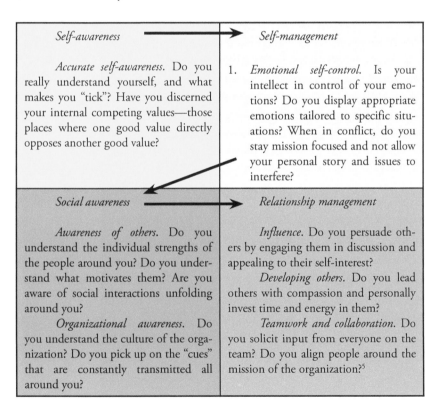

Self-awareness	*Self-management*
Accurate self-awareness. Do you really understand yourself, and what makes you "tick"? Have you discerned your internal competing values—those places where one good value directly opposes another good value?	1. *Emotional self-control.* Is your intellect in control of your emotions? Do you display appropriate emotions tailored to specific situations? When in conflict, do you stay mission focused and not allow your personal story and issues to interfere?
Social awareness	*Relationship management*
Awareness of others. Do you understand the individual strengths of the people around you? Do you understand what motivates them? Are you aware of social interactions unfolding around you? *Organizational awareness.* Do you understand the culture of the organization? Do you pick up on the "cues" that are constantly transmitted all around you?	*Influence.* Do you persuade others by engaging them in discussion and appealing to their self-interest? *Developing others.* Do you lead others with compassion and personally invest time and energy in them? *Teamwork and collaboration.* Do you solicit input from everyone on the team? Do you align people around the mission of the organization?[5]

---

[5]   Adapted from Daniel Goleman, *Emotional Intelligence*

Smart people, people with all kinds of degrees from all the best places, often make poor leaders, not all of them, but many of them. And the reason for this is that this latter group of folks, though knowing all kinds of facts about many areas of life, lacks the kind of self-awareness that would allow them to manage themselves, leading to social awareness and the ability to manage relationships appropriately.

Researchers had managers in one group give negative feedback on performance to their direct reports but had them give it with positive nonverbals—nods and smiles. Then these researchers had managers give feedback to subordinates that was positive about their performance, but with negative nonverbals—frowns and narrow eyes. Guess what? Both groups ignored the verbal evaluations and only reacted to the nonverbals; the positive performers ended up feeling bad about what they'd done, and the bad performers feeling good.

What this means for a leader is this: You can give content all day to those you lead. You can tell them what they're doing well or poorly. But that counts for very little. What really counts is the *way* you deliver it. And if you're not aware of how you're coming across, you could be giving all kinds of messages that you had no idea you were giving.

And that's one major reason there's so much bad leading and bad management out there in the world. Leaders often have no idea how they're coming across to people, why people do not want to work with them, and why they can get so little good performance out of their people. Even leaders who more often than not are effective have little or any idea as to why they've been successful. Frequently they focus on a particular trait that they judge to be the critical determinant, while missing completely those elements that truly make them successful.

Understanding the impact you have on those you lead is critical to success as a leader and a key component of self-awareness. And yet, few leaders seem to have much of a grasp of this attribute.

The Three Aspects of Self-Awareness

There are three aspects of self-awareness that are critical for a person on the journey to being well defined:

The first aspect of self-awareness is understanding how we have been uniquely created—our particular bent if you will. Some people have called this the element. Others term it our "sweet spot." Still others call it our unique talent pool or our hedgehog principle. Whatever you call it, it involves the hardwiring internal to each of us that makes us uniquely who we are.[6]

We've found it to be tremendously helpful to begin figuring ourselves out starting with focusing on the positive—our unique strengths' makeup. So often people have told us that they have little or no idea what they are truly good at and what they are passionate about. Obviously, if we aren't clear on our unique wiring, and where our strengths and talents lie, we will not have a clear understanding of ourselves or feel comfortable in our skin as we move about our lives from day to day.

The most important tool we use in this self-discovery endeavor, based on Gallup's Strengthsfinder©, is the concept of intentional difference©. We will not delve into this extensively here, since this has been discussed adequately elsewhere.[7]

The well-defined leader is one who spends a preponderance of his/her time functioning in his/her intentional difference. This ID, as we call it, represents that convergence of our talents turned into strengths where all of our faculties are combined in a harmonious order. When we are functioning in our ID, we are extremely focused, lost in the moment. We perform at our peak, getting lost in the process and losing a sense of the passage of time. We can work for hours

---

[6] This is the nature part of nature-nurture debate. And to arbitrarily separate these is problematic, but instructive to understand forces at play. Part of us is innate and present at birth (nature), and part is molded by our surroundings (nurture). But these also interact and shape one another, making the distinction difficult to impossible.

[7] See *Intentional Difference* by Ken Tucker and www.intentionaldifference.me

and are actually energized rather than depleted by the experience. At these times, we are authentically centered in the true sense of ourselves—we are well defined.

Obviously, those who can combine their career with their ID will be those who function in those careers at the highest levels, at the same time maintaining a sense of accomplishment and fulfillment that unfortunately few of us realize. Those who are rarely if ever in their ID will usually find themselves depleted. These folks may also turn to artificial stimulants to produce the synthetic high that ID naturally produces (although these artificial means often lead to addictions and a host of associated problems).

It should be noted that there is absolutely no perfect job. Everyone must spend a certain amount of time outside of his ID. Unfortunately, the tendency is to default to the sweet spot whenever possible, often leaving those other responsibilities ignored or poorly performed. Or people become trapped in jobs that capture practically none of their ID. Often these people long for the weekends when they can plunge into ID endeavors.

The second aspect that is critical is our own personal story. Each of us has come from a particular background. We grew up in a family. In that family we were a particular gender and occupied a particular birth order. Our parents exhibited certain traits, habits, and behaviors toward us and the world. We grew up in a community that had a special DNA, and that community molded us in certain ways. We had seminal events in our lives, with special people entering our lives at critical moments, for good or for ill. The sum total of all of these life events I call our unique story or narrative out of which each of us now lives. We use this unique story as a "pair of glasses" to give us perspective on everyone and all that is going on around us. This story can also been understood as a "map" to show us the way forward.

Robert E. Lee is a good example. He has come from one of the most prestigious families of Virginia. But that prestige has been significantly sullied. His father, a revolutionary cavalry commander and hero, governor of Virginia and friend of George Washington, had owed money to everyone from Washington on down due to bad business decisions. He married the heiress of a vast Virginia fortune and proceeded to squander her wealth on failed business ventures. He died penniless, leaving his family to be rescued financially by his wife's family. Added to this, one of Robert's older half brothers was accused of, at best, abuse, and, at worst, incest. He had taken in the teenaged sister of his ill wife and proceeded to impregnate her. Virginia was scandalized. The family name was dragged through the mud, and arguably the task of restoring that name had fallen to Robert.

There are numerous other aspects of Robert's story that are pertinent to his actions. (A good example is his father's flamboyance in combat, mirrored by J. E. B. Stuart, who functioned as a son to Lee. Also was the fact that Robert had married the only child of George Washington's adopted son, making him, at least in his mind, the heir to Washington's legacy). Suffice it to say, the family story that shaped him growing up was critical to the person he became as an adult, and understanding this shaping process could have proved invaluable to him when he was making critical decisions.

George Meade's family is in certain ways similar. His father is a Philadelphia merchant who had fallen on hard times due to bad investments, which evidently had caused his untimely death. Young George watched his family's story unfold, and one might speculate that he was haunted by the specter of his penniless father. Unlike Robert's father, who lost his money to unfettered profligacy, George's father lost his money from a combination of bad luck and bad judgment. Circumstances can turn against a person, even with the most careful planning, so a healthy dose of caution is always required. It would have been helpful for George to recognize these tendencies when he took command and was forced to make decisions at critical turning points in battles and in the war.

The third aspect of self-awareness is the culture that surrounds us. Our thoughts, our emotions, our beliefs, and ultimately our behavior are shaped by culture. None of us can escape these forces, and getting a handle on them can prove very helpful.

Robert E. Lee is from the South, but not just the South. He's from Virginia, the colony to which cavaliers escaped when Charles I was beheaded. It is the colony set up as a business venture, not as a reli-

gious enclave, and the accumulation of wealth (principally land) is paramount. People are very aware of who's who in the pecking order according to how much land they possess. Added to this, the South is enamored of Sir Walter Scott and the dashing cavalier wielding his weapon in mortal combat, struggling in a just cause. There is little tolerance for defense when it comes to warfare, though arguably a defensive posture, given the enormous landmass the South represents and the lack of industrial capacity, would have been the smarter course of action throughout the war and at Gettysburg. Lee is shaped by his culture. But the offensive orientation is one important determining factor in his decision-making.

Lee takes over what he refashions and renames the Army of Northern Virginia. Joe Johnston, his predecessor, was the consummate defensive-minded fighter, which does not align well with the expectations of the South. Lee assumes command when Johnston is wounded in defending Richmond in June 1862. Lee immediately puts his audacious offensive stamp on the organization (an offensive defense), reorganizing the units and immediately hurling them against the Union army. Though virtually winning none of the contests the next seven days, and running up enormous casualties, he won the hearts of the southern people, who understood that this strategy would ultimately win them independence. He also drove George McClellan's Army of the Potomac back to the shores of the James River where it was no longer a potent offensive force.

George Meade inherited an army that was fashioned by his predecessor George McClellan. McClellan named it the Army of the Potomac. McClellan is a masterful organizer and is able to put the army in shape organizationally. But he is a poor battlefield commander, who demands that everything must be just so (an impossibility once the firing begins), and as a consequence is extremely cautious when faced with an opposing threat. McClellan is the consummate paradoxical personality—on one hand, pompous in the extreme, while, on the other, paralyzed with self-doubt on the battlefield. As stated, Meade has also watched one commander after another micromanaged from Washington and cashiered when the inevitable failure has occurred. Meade is not in any way ready to take unreasonable chances.

The Three Aspects Combined

Now let's put together these three aspects of self-awareness to get a better handle on how leadership actually unfolds.

For Lee, he comes from a prominent though sullied family and feels responsible to reclaim the family name. Added to this, he lives in a region and a time when daring, slashing offense is the ticket for effective military leadership during wartime. And one can conclude that these factors fit right in with how he personally is wired:

   ✓   *Exhibit audacity to the point of recklessness.*
   ✓   *Seize the initiative and never relinquish it.*
   ✓   *Be extremely aggressive—the best defense is a determined offense.*

For George Meade, it is quite the opposite. He hails from a family where bad judgment joined with bad luck had brought disaster. The administration in Washington gave mixed messages—hit the rebels hard, but take great caution to keep the nation's capital safe, and don't do anything stupid. And he had inherited an army where commander after commander has fallen from grace for attempting to operate effectively under the watchful eye of a distrustful administration. This undoubtedly had played right into his natural propensities:

   ✓   *Always be cautious.*
   ✓   *Allow the other side to take the initiative, and react to it as the situation unfolds.*
   ✓   *Get consensus from your subordinate commanders, to shore up your own doubt and irresolution.*

A leader axiom that is often ignored is this: Your greatest strength is also your greatest weakness. It all depends on the context in which you employ your strength. *Consider J. E. B. Stuart, the brash, flamboyant, colorful, risk-taking cavalry commander under Lee. These particular qualities of Stuart suited him well, winning him victories and acclaim time and again, but not always. These traits also contributed to the disaster that was Gettysburg for the southern cause. If Stuart had been more self-aware, he'd have realized that his brashness could often get him into trouble, the brashness trumping better judgment.[8] As the two armies were converging on Gettysburg, Lee was essentially "blind" due to Stuart's impetuous foray into Maryland inadvertently placing the Union army between himself and the Army of Northern Virginia, thus rendering the cavalry incapable of supplying Lee with critical information.*

Role Versus Self

One final point with regard to the well-defined leader is as follows: these well-defined leaders we've been discussing are people who not only understand their role, but maintain the distinction between their understanding of who they are as a person and who they are within their roles.

Role and responsibilities are often used interchangeably when describing a position of authority. Responsibility has to do with *tasks* that need to be effectively accomplished. A role is about the *purpose* of the position. What is the purpose of the position of authority I have been given?

Corps commanders both North and South at Gettysburg had their own corps for which they were responsible. They also were part of the leadership team of Meade and Lee. What makes this dual responsibility (to the corps and to the army) difficult and confusing is the fact that at times what is decided at the army senior leadership table may directly conflict with the aims and goals of a particular corps. In other words, the corps commander, tasked with the safety and success of the overall army, may have to vote for something he knows will harm the goals he has for his corps.

---

[8]   Understanding the "enemy" force and the environment in which you both operate are also critical factors in effective leadership. The most self-aware leader can still fail, due to a stronger or more skillful opposing force or just bad luck—the weather interferes, the terrain favors the other side, etc.

For example, on the second day of battle at Gettysburg, W. S. Hancock realized he had to detach his first division under General Caldwell (which happened to be stationed closest to the crumbling III Corps) to rescue Sickles from the impossible scrape in which he found himself. This weakened Hancock's own corps and position, but it was the only prudent course of action given the deteriorating situation down to the south of his line.

The question each person must ask of him or herself is this: are the actions I am taking or the decisions I am making fulfilling the purpose of my role or undermining my purpose? When you are entrusted with a new role, you cannot assume you understand the purpose of the role. Learning the deepest purpose of the role takes time, and when you have a role that carries with it enormous responsibility, as each leader has, you must be focused on learning the purpose. Second, and critically important to understand, is the role you have is not who you are—it does not define who you are as a person. When people fuse their identity with their role, it's very difficult to handle feedback, very difficult to understand the feedback you are getting and very difficult to learn how to use your talents in the service of the role. Any combination of talents will allow anyone to be successful as long as he or she uses their talents in the service of the role and not simply in the service of self.

The Battle

As dawn broke on July 1, the first day of battle, Lee had three corps strung out in southern Pennsylvania. His lead element, the II under Dick Ewell, had passed through Gettysburg a few days earlier and was now heading toward Harrisburg, the capital of the state. A. P. Hill's III Corps was in the middle, concentrating around Cashtown just west of Gettysburg. James Longstreet's I Corps was trailing behind the first two corps. Even as his army spread out in enemy territory probing for opportunity, Lee was essentially "blind" to the enemy's whereabouts. His cavalry commander, J. E. B. Stuart, had taken it upon himself to ride to the east of the Army of the Potomac, thus placing that army between himself and Lee. Stuart's indispensable ability to be the "eyes" of Lee's army was thus lost to Lee for several critical days.

Lee did not realize that the Union army was coming fast on his heels. Lee had hoped, when the time was right, to turn his army on the Army of the Potomac and beat each element of that army in detail as it came up to meet him. But where were these elements of the Federal army? How far away? How close to one another were the various enemy units? These questions he could not answer.[9]

General Meade, on the other hand, just placed in command of the Union army, had found a defensive position back in Maryland he hoped to assume and coax Lee into attacking him in this position. But his I Corps commander John Reynolds had already pushed up into southern Pennsylvania and was preparing to meet Lee's army there.

In warfare, the best laid plans usually come to naught the moment the bullets start flying.

Take Action

- Go to the website http://intentionaldifference.me and take the assessment to discover your intentional difference (ID©).
- Look at the chart below. In the first column, list the significant times in your life story. Then, think of and list the specific events that happened during each significant period. Next, write in the people who were important to you during those events, then the emotional impact that each event had on you. Last, write in the decisions you made as a consequence of these events.

---

[9]   A scout for General Longstreet had supplied Lee with some information, but it was incomplete.

Significant period	Events	People	Emotional impact	Decisions made

- Take out a sheet of paper and draw two large circles. In the left circle, write ID. Below that, list the areas of responsibility that you routinely perform that align with your ID. In the other circle, write non-ID, and list those areas you routinely perform that do not fall within your ID. If you like, you can put a percentage of time after each area, and then add up the percentages for each circle. This will give you a sense of how much of your time is actually spent performing in your ID and how much time is spent outside of your ID.

Chapter 2

How Do I Build Trust?

Most leaders realize that trust is foundational to their success. If the people they lead don't trust them, how can they be expected to follow? Even in the military, where there could be forced compliance, leaders need to be trusted in order to exact the highest performance from those they lead.

The Battle

Robert E. Lee and George Meade both rode into Pennsylvania at the head of their respective armies, each in a very different place in their relationship to those armies. Lee had led his men for over a year and met with success after success on the battlefield. His men had come to trust him implicitly. When he rides past his marching troops, his men stop, take off their hats, and stand worshipfully.

By contrast, George Meade had just been elevated to command a few days before. He is basically unknown by all but those in the V Corps. When he rides past his troops, few recognize him, much less acknowledge him. He is an unknown quantity and will have to earn that trust over time.

Basically, by sheer accident, the battle of Gettysburg was unfolding on that first day of July. General John Reynolds' (I Corps Union commander) cavalry screen under John Buford had been feeling its way north over the Maryland border into Pennsylvania searching for the

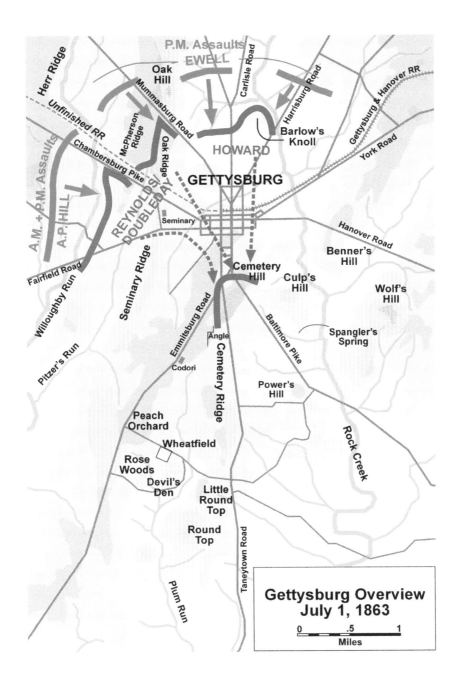

Gettysburg Overview
July 1, 1863

0   .5   1
Miles

Confederate army. These horsemen had come to the outskirts of the little hamlet of Gettysburg on the last day of June and noted what appeared to be southern infantry off to the west. Buford, an excellent cavalry leader, had taken it upon himself to deploy his three thousand troops on the ridges just west of the town and wait for the situation to develop. He could see the excellent defensive position offered just south of the town including Culp's Hill, Cemetery Hill and its ridge extending south, and the two Round Tops further south. He figured if he could delay southern forces long enough out to the west of town, Reynolds, in the forefront of the rest of the Union army, could come and deploy on these excellent defensive positions before Lee had time to do the same.

General Buford also sent word to General Reynolds as to what he had seen and what he was subsequently doing. Early in the morning of July 1, the lead southern elements of A. P. Hill's (III Corps) second division under Henry Heth came pushing down the road heading east out of Cashtown toward Gettysburg. They were seeking supplies in the town and had been mistakenly told (J. E. B. Stuart the southern cavalry commander was not available to supply dependable information, necessitating a reconnaissance in force) that there were only local militia there that could easily be swept aside.

At 7:30 that July 1 morning, the first shots rang out as northern and southern forces began to engage one another. What was to become the largest and fiercest battle ever fought on the American continent had commenced.

The Face of Trust

I have said that the truly effective leader is the well-defined leader. This well-defined leader is one who has a great deal of (and ever-deepening) self-awareness and good personal boundaries. As a result, the well-defined leader is able to first trust himself. This leader has a good sense of personal strengths and weaknesses. This leader knows his talents, and he has developed these talents into strengths. He knows when to employ these strengths and when these strengths might be a detriment. He has a good sense of what it's like to be on the other side of him—how his actions and attitudes are perceived by and impact other people.

It is this well-defined leader who will be able to most effectively build trust in his people. Being well defined, this person is internally aligned—he is able to match his words with his actions. This is directly opposite of the person we say "speaks out of both sides of his mouth." It is this congruence (actions match words) that is the key element in building trust. Let's unpack this further. This concept seems so simple and straightforward. But it is a principle that, in coaching leader after leader, I see violated time and again.

To begin our discussion on trust, take a look at these elements that make for a fully functional organization, each point building on the one preceding it:

The functional organization[10]

1. Trusts one another
2. Engages in conflict around ideas
3. Commits to decisions and plans of action
4. Holds one another accountable for delivering against those plans
5. Focuses on the achievement of collective results

Notice that trusting one another is the foundation of a functional organization of any size. Once trust is established, the team can enter into appropriate, constructive conflict, without fear that it will turn destructive.

Trust has to do with a willingness on people's part to be vulnerable within the team and share in the team's ups and downs. It's an openness about mistakes and weaknesses. Teams that lack trust are unable to engage in unfiltered and passionate disagreement around the mission of the organization. Instead, they resort to veiled discussions and guarded comments.

---

[10] Adapted from Patrick Lencioni, *The Five Dysfunctions of a Team*

Once you have a trusting team, you can have honest disagreements that lead to decisions and plans of action *to which people are actually committed*. So much of what I see in organizations is compliance ("I'll do what you ask, but my heart's not in it"), but very little commitment. Commitment arises only after each member of a team has been able to wrestle with the initiatives that are presented, offer their disagreements, and grapple with all of the alternatives before arriving at a decision. Once that occurs, the team can hold one another accountable, because there is a shared sense of ownership in the decision.

Trust → Disagree → Commit to decisions → Develop mutual accountability → Focus on the achievements created

---

In my coaching/consulting life, I coach several people in the federal government who are responsible for over ten thousand people. That's a lot of people to direct. What I tell these leaders is actually they are not directing ten thousand people; they are directing the eight or ten people who are their direct reports. Those are the people whose trust they must win and lead effectively. *For Lee, it was Longstreet, A. P. Hill, Dick Ewell, and J. E. B. Stuart. For Meade, it was Reynolds, Hancock, Sickles, Sykes, Sedgwick, Howard, and Slocum.* Unfortunately, for leaders of large organizations, distractions and interruptions run high, and the ability to keep one's eye on the main thing becomes extremely difficult. It is also difficult for leaders to understand when their words no longer match their behavior, thus setting in motion the erosion of trust.

How Is Trust Established?

Let's look at the building blocks that are critical to the growth of trust:

I am well-defined and internally aligned (congruent)—what I say equals what I do.

I am consistent (a direct result of being internally aligned).
I can be depended on.
I am predictable.
When I'm wrong, I admit it and own it.

Let's begin with predictability—you're able to *predict* in advance what I will do. That's because I'm *consistent*. I do the same thing, over and over again, free from variation or contradiction. But I could do the same *wrong* thing over and over. So that means I have to be *dependable*: I get the same positive result over and over again from the person or organization. And as we've said, the whole thing rests on *congruence*—I'm well defined and internally aligned. Therefore what I say I believe and value matches how I behave.

Note now the very bottom—*when I'm wrong, I admit it and own it*. In all arenas of leadership, we have heard over and over again the inability of the leader to own his or her mistakes. Blame shifting has become a leadership art form. Jim Collins explains this in his book, *From Good to Great*. He states that for the level five leader (well-defined as I label this person), when there is acclaim, the leader looks out the window, downplaying his part in the success and sharing the spotlight with his subordinates. When there is a problem, this leader looks in the mirror, embracing the responsibility.

This was no less true during the battle of Gettysburg. During and especially after the conflict, general after general sought to vindicate his own actions, while casting blame on fellow generals for poor performance. General Longstreet is a case in point. After the war, he did the unpardonable sin of criticizing Lee for his performance at Gettysburg. Those who worshipped Lee then took it upon themselves to blame Longstreet for the lost battle, misstating fact after fact to justify their positions.

The arena in which being well-defined and congruent is on display, and indeed, where it is validated is in the area of communication. Indeed, it is in communication where trust will either be won or lost. So let's take a close look at communication and see how this critical activity can either make or break us as we go about building trust.

Let's begin with the premise that a person cannot *not* communicate. We are constantly in the act of communicating—giving and receiving messages. Communication is difficult because we communicate through different channels, and we register other people's communication differently. Note the picture of the two people communicating.

Notice that the woman is saying something to the man. She has a particular intent: "John, I need your help?"

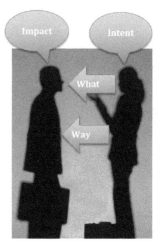

Hopefully, what she intends by her message equals the impact of her message on John. But that isn't always the case. That's because communication has more than one channel. My content (what) also carries relational signals in the *way* that I say things—body language, tone of voice, and facial expressions.

When I say something to you, my words carry one message that you hear consciously (the *what* of my message), and my body language and behavior communicates another message (the *way* of my message). This *way* is usually communicated by me and registered by you unconsciously. What that means is that I can say one thing ("I really value women and their contribution in the organization") and at the same time contradict that message by my body language or behavior. (I never seek out women for their opinions and tend to only hear and value contributions by men.) Whenever there is a discrepancy between what I say verbally and how I act nonverbally (a double message), the verbal message is rejected (actions speak louder than words). Also, trust in the communicator is diminished or destroyed.

We are often the very worst candidates to monitor incongruence *in ourselves*. When our minds experience ourselves being incongruent, anxiety is generated, and the first order of business for our minds is to reduce the anxiety. This often occurs by merely telling ourselves a lie, that there really is no discrepancy between what I just said to you and how I'm acting. Consequently we're very bad at monitoring our own incongruence and need the help of an outsider whom we trust.

Cognitive Dissonance

We are complex as people, and within this complexity, there are competing values that are constantly at war with each other. So how are we able to not only survive but move forward as individuals? We can very well go around with our minds tied up in knots, what is now termed cognitive dissonance. It would be too confusing, and we'd never be able to make any decisions, one part of our mind pulling us in one direction, the other in another.

Our minds yearn for harmony, consistency, and alignment. And yet, as we have seen, competing values lurk within each of us, threatening to throw us into disharmony and cognitive chaos.

Our minds become dissonant when we hold two contradictory beliefs or values simultaneously—one idea implying the opposite of another. For example, a belief in animal rights could be interpreted as inconsistent with eating meat or wearing fur. The contradiction leads to dissonance, our minds experiencing an embarrassment, shame, guilt, anger, embarrassment, anxiety, and stress.

When our minds are dissonant and under stress as a result, we have two options:

1. Change our values, attitudes, beliefs, and behavior.
2. Justify or rationalize our values, attitudes, beliefs, and behaviors.

It is much more difficult to change our values, attitudes, beliefs, and behaviors. It's far easier to just rationalize away discrepancies (we tell ourselves a lie: *there is no contradiction here*).

A powerful cause of dissonance revolves around how we view ourselves, our <u>self-concept</u>: "I am a good person" or "I made the right decision." Anxiety rises with the possibility of having made a bad decision. (I am a good person. How could I have made a bad decision?) To clear up the dissonance created and the subsequent anxiety, we rationalize, telling ourselves the reasons or justifications to support our choice. A person who just spent more than his allotted budget on a new truck may justify this purchase pointing to all the weekend projects for which the truck will be useful. This belief may or may not be true, but it would likely reduce dissonance and make the person feel better. Dissonance can also lead to <u>confirmation bias</u>, the <u>denial</u> of disconfirming evidence, and other notions our minds concoct to defend ourselves.

All of us strive to make sense out of contradictory ideas and lead lives that are, *at least in our own minds*, consistent and meaningful. In order to keep our self-esteem bubbling along in high gear, our minds are forced to clear up all the discrepancies. The operation is similar to a thermostat. The thermostat in your house kicks on when the thermometer reaches a certain point. The same with our minds, when the dissonance reaches a certain point, rationalization kicks in to regulate the "temperature."

Our convictions about the person we are carry us through the day, and we constantly interpret the things that happen to us through the filter of those core beliefs. When they are violated, even by a good experience, it causes anxiety that must be reduced.

What is important to remember is the fact that leaders who are consistent, who are congruent, whose lives mirror the words they speak, are the leaders who build trust in their followers because those followers can rely on what the leader says.

Building Trust

You can either build trust with those you lead or allow cynicism to breed.

Unfortunately, it is easy for leaders to moan about problems in their organization and for cynicism to creep into any organization. So let's talk about your own personal team.

Remember our first principle: the effective leader is one who is well defined and is self-aware. When it comes to building trust, it is critical to have a really good handle on yourself—where your strengths lie, where you are vulnerable (we're back to understanding yourself). Let's look at the specifics of this to see exactly how this works.

When the leader is well-defined and congruent, he can then go about doing the following. These are activities that build strong trust in those who are led. Note that each one of these often is counterintuitive as to how people normally assume leadership practices should unfold.

Admits weaknesses or mistakes. The well-defined leader who knows himself well is not threatened by admitting to weaknesses and mistakes. "I'm so sorry, I blew it" is a phrase that comes easy. This leader also, because he knows himself well, not only understands where his weaknesses lie but is able to speak of these freely so that others have that understanding.

The first day of battle at Gettysburg saw one mistake after another. The first was Henry Heth (A. P. Hill's III Corps) stumbling into battle, initially with Union cavalry, then with the elite of the Union army, the Iron Brigade of the I Corps. He had been told not to bring on the engagement, and yet that is precisely what he did. Following his mistake, there were other southern mistakes that compounded the first. The most egregious was Robert Rodes coming in on the Union right flank from Oak Hill as Ewell's II Corps lead division. Rodes saw what he thought was the perfect opportunity to roll up the Union line, so he sent in his two weakest brigades under O'Neal and Iverson without reconnaissance (assessing the situation) only to see both brigades ambushed and routed.

Long after the battle was fought, and even after the Civil War ended, commanders on both sides justified their own mistakes and blame-shifted. It is difficult to find in the writings of commanders of those terrible days in July admissions of error and mistakes. Even Lee, who after Pickett's Charge stated, "It's all my fault," began to equivocate as time passed, stating other's errors that had led to the defeat.

Asks for help. Because the well-defined leader understands and articulates weaknesses and mistakes, she is able to reach out and ask for help. For some leaders, this going into the "one-down" position is very difficult. Often these people feel very vulnerable in this position and refuse to assume it. "If I ask for help, people will assume I'm weak and will no longer follow me." But this is also a part of self-understanding. (It is very difficult for me to ask for help. But it is also critical that I do this, in order to maintain the integrity of the organization.)

On the day before the battle, General John Buford took his cavalry division west of Gettysburg and stationed on the ridges to meet the oncoming Confederate army. He knew he could not hold the next day more than a couple of hours. So he immediately sent back to John Reynolds for help. Reynolds hurried forward while asking Meade for assistance. As the battle unfolded, commander after commander asked one another for assistance as the tide of battle ebbed and flowed.

Accepts feedback and input. Once help is solicited, the well-defined leader is able to accept the feedback and input offered. This may seem obvious, but certain people, though able to articulate weaknesses and ask for help, find themselves paralyzed when it comes to accepting the help offered. And in fact, one critical aspect of leadership is the ability to face reality. Ron Heifetz details three realities that must be faced:

- First, what we say we stand for (our values) and the gaps between those values and how we actually behave.
- Second, the reality of the skills and talents of our company—and the gaps between those resources and what the market demands.
- Third, the opportunities the future hold and the gaps between those opportunities and our ability to capitalize on them.[11]

Lee was probably in the position of being unable to accept feedback and input as he followed his lead division toward Gettysburg on the first day

---

[11]   Ron Heifetz, "The Leader of the Future." *Fast Company*

of the battle (and consequently compromised in his ability to interrogate the realities that faced him). Having almost by happenstance won that first day as his legions had come onto the field at the right moment in the right place, there is strong evidence that he was feeling invincible and that his troops could accomplish the impossible.

Such a mindset runs counter to a leader who is able to accept feedback and input from anyone, especially those who will point out the "elephant in the room." Once the Union troops had dug in on Cemetery Hill and down the ridge that extends south from there, the position became more and more formidable. Longstreet saw this and, as Lee's senior subordinate, told him again and again that attacking the Union position would prove futile. Lee would hear none of this and persisted in his delusions until the end of the third day when his men were disastrously repulsed in Pickett's Charge.

Gives each other the benefit of the doubt. The well-defined leader is able to give people the benefit of the doubt. This actually flies in the face of what is often the unconscious automatic response when we see someone doing something of which we disapprove—assign immediate negative intent. "I know why you got that report to me late. You wanted me to look bad." This assigning intention, like communication itself, is a ubiquitous activity that is highly destructive to achieving and maintaining trust. It is impossible to trust someone when they assign negative intentions to that person's behavior. Rather than assigning intent, the far better course is to give the benefit of a doubt and inquire as to motive. "You got me the report late. Can you tell me what happened?"

A serious confrontation happened on Cemetery Hill as the afternoon unfolded on the first day of battle. O. O. Howard's XI Corps had rushed north through the town and out onto the fields to the right of the splintered I Corps. There, Howard's corps had been shattered as Ewell's Confederates had descended on him at the exact worst moment, crushing Howard's lines. His men had streamed back through town and up onto Cemetery Hill where Howard had prudently posted his reserve division. As Howard was digging in, Winfield S. Hancock rode up with orders from Meade placing Hancock in overall charge of this wing of the army.

Back then, seniority in command was everything, and Howard was more senior to Hancock.

Howard at first was humiliated, pleading to Meade, "It has mortified me and will disgrace me. Please inform me frankly if you disapprove of my conduct today, that I may know what to do."[12] All of that aside, Howard's performance was remarkable in that, in the face of overwhelming stress, he carefully plotted a fallback maneuver to a defensive position that proved essential to victory. Rather than impute malicious intent to Hancock, Howard acceded to Hancock and continued to build a strong defense of Cemetery Hill, which proved crucial to the success of Union forces at Gettysburg.

Takes risks in offering feedback. Giving feedback to people can be risky, both to self and to the relationship. Often feedback, as in the above point, involves ascribing negative intent to other people's behavior. This activity of negative intent usually has more to say about the assigner than the person to whom the intent is ascribed. But honest constructive feedback can be very helpful both to the person and to the organization. There are always risks, however, to offering feedback. Recipients may reject what is offered, while imputing bad motives on the feedback giver. But this possibility is diminished when the offerer is well defined with a reputation of giving feedback that is constructive and centered on the enhancement of the person and the organization.

One of the oft-forgotten heroes of the Gettysburg battle is George "Pap" Greene, a northern general who, at sixty-two, is one of the oldest commanders on the field. He had come to the battle as the first day's sun was setting, taking up position on Culp's Hill just below Evergreen Cemetery where Howard was digging in. On the second day of battle, General George Meade shifted almost the entire XII Corps, of which Greene was a brigade commander, from the Union right to strengthen the left flank, which was under heavy attack. Greene's lone brigade of 1,350 New Yorkers (five regiments) was left to defend a one-half-mile line on

---

[12] Being removed from command in this way could have been seen as a severe rebuke for a commander's inability to perform adequately.

Culp's Hill when an entire Confederate division attacked. Fortunately, Greene had previously demonstrated good sense (as befits a civil engineer) by insisting that his troops construct strong field fortifications, despite a lack of interest in doing so from his division commander, Geary, and corps commander, Maj. Gen. Henry W. Slocum.[13] In Greene's finest moment of the war, his feedback to his superiors and his preparations proved decisive and his brigade held off multiple attacks for hours. His ability to take a risk in the face of possible scorn and rebuke from his superiors contributed to saving the Union right flank.

Focuses time and energy on issues, not politics. Well-defined leaders understand those issues that will enhance the organization and tend to spend the majority of their time focused on these. Politics swirl around all organizations and certainly have to be monitored. But the self-aware leader understands when he has handled contentious issues appropriately rather than sinking down into political haggling that is usually more centered on personalities than on the good of the organization as a whole.

The Army of the Potomac proved to be a hotbed of political intrigue. Men at the top of the command structure continually under-cut one another in their reach for personal advancement. Officers had gone behind commanders' backs directly to Lincoln and Secretary of War Stanton to complain of the shortcomings of their peers and superiors.

Henry Hunt was a general who was able to rise above the intrigue to effectively perform his duties. Throughout the war, Hunt proved again and again to be somewhat of a genius at the proper use of artillery during battle. Maj. Gen. George G. Meade had considerably more respect for Hunt than former commander Hooker did and not only gave him great latitude in directing the artillery but also used him on occasion as his personal representative. For example, on July 2, Meade sent Hunt to visit III Corps commander Maj. Gen. Daniel E. Sickles in an attempt to get his defensive lines to conform to orders. (Sickles' insubordinate move-

---

[13]   Digging fortifications on a battle was understood to impede proper handling of troops, and it was feared this would also lead to poor morale when men were crouching behind earthworks rather than standing erect and fighting.

ment from Cemetery Ridge, where he had been ordered to defend, to the Peach Orchard caused considerable difficulty for the entire Union defense.) Hunt was unable to influence the irascible political general, but his masterful analysis of terrain and placement of batteries on the ridge were important factors in the Union's eventual success on the second day.

Hunt's handling of the artillery was conspicuous in the repulse of Pickett's Charge on July 3. With the Union line on Cemetery Ridge under massive bombardment, Hunt was able to resist command pressure that would have expended all his ammunition in fruitless counterbattery fire, reserving sufficient amounts for antipersonnel fire in the attack he knew was coming. His orders to cease firing (despite the strong orders of fiery II Corps commander Maj. Gen. Winfield S. Hancock) fooled the Confederates into thinking his batteries were destroyed and triggered their disastrous charge. His concealed placement of Lt. Col. Freeman McGilvery's batteries north of Little Round Top caused massive casualties in the infantry assault. Hunt proved to be a leader who could focus on issues without himself becoming embroiled and detoured by the politics of the organization.

Shares in the team's ups and downs. One glaring problem with the preponderance of leadership across the organizational spectrum is the propensity of leaders to be first in line to grab the benefits of leadership, while leaving the leftovers to those they lead. *Lee was a leader who tended to be last in line, insisting on sharing the fate of his army. When offered comfortable house rather than his tent for his head-quarters, he almost always chose his tent. When given food by the adoring public, he sent it to the hospitals. And this was from a man in his upper fifties who was also in ill health a good part of the war. His men knew that he was choosing to share their fate, and that made them adore him all the more.*

Trust and the Principle-Based Organization

With all the internal intrigue that had unfolded during the previous two years in the senior leadership of the Army of the Potomac, George Meade had his work cut out for him winning the trust of his direct reports and the army writ large. When it came to values[14], undoubtedly most of his senior team of generals figured that his primary value was his own personal advancement, not what was good for the army. This principal value was the one that apparently had motivated most if not all of his predecessors to one degree or another.

Robert E. Lee did not have the trust mountain to climb with his men. Not only had he led them for a year from victory to victory, he had eschewed all the trappings of leadership to share his men's lot. He had truly "eaten last," as Simon Sinek (Leaders Eat Last) points out about the successful leaders, who win the hearts of their followers. In biological terms, leaders get the first pick of food and other spoils, but at a cost. When danger is present, the group expects the leader to mitigate all threats even at the expense of his personal well-being. At Gettysburg, senior leadership would suffer fearful casualties precisely because they tended to lead from up front and receive an inordinate amount of incoming fire. Understanding this deep-seated expectation is the key difference between someone who is just an "authority" and a true "leader (to be discussed shortly)."

Human nature draws each one of us to default to self-interest and value those things most advantageous to self over other considerations (e.g., advantages to the mission of the organization). This is seen again and again in leader after leader, especially those who have not been successful. That's why the leader who puts others above himself stands out. These are the ones who are most readily followed and trusted. People know that these leaders are looking out for the good of the organization.

A discussion of trust goes hand in hand with a discussion of values or the principles that govern our behavior. Values are like force fields that protect the organization. When the leaders demonstrate a coherent set of principles consistently over time (they're congruent), these values permeate the system and influence all those who come in contact with that organization. The principles are not only spoken of frequently; they are lived constantly. When a person comes in

---

[14]   The terms value and principle are used interchangeably.

contact with anyone from the organization no matter the position, that person experiences the whole organization—for good or for ill.

What is critical about trust is having a set of principles (what matters most in the organization), making sure that my life and subsequent behavior are aligned with those principles (congruent), making decisions based on these values (my operating or decision-making values, which often conflict with core values), and judging performance based on these values.

When organizations are misaligned, trust is destroyed, and cynicism rises. Misalignment can be compared to sails that are not properly trimmed. This creates a drag on the boat as it moves forward. Take a look at Enron's core values:

> *Communication*—we have an obligation to communicate.
> *Respect*—we treat others as we would like to be treated.
> *Integrity*—we work with customers and prospects openly, honestly, and sincerely.
> *Excellence*—we are satisfied with nothing less than the very best in everything we do. (*Enron,* Annual Report, 2000, p. 29)

Now the disgraced leadership of that failed company is held in derision because of their utter disregard for these principles. That's what incongruence looks like. Obviously, the leadership of Enron posted those values, but when it came to making key decisions about the direction of the company, those values were discarded, and a whole new set of values was put on the table, beginning with this: *make all the money we can, any way we can, no matter whom we hurt.*

So it's critical for the leaders within an organization to be aligned with the principles of the organization (only truly achieved when those leaders are well defined). Now the question arises: how do we actually get people within the organization to align themselves with the values of the organization?

First, you need to remember the following: stating a set of values and actually *practicing* a set of values are two different things. Our statement of values is all too often the "right" thing to value. In other words, organizations say they value people, they value honesty, and they value customer service. But what do these values look like when they are actually lived out in real time?

When leaders actually have to make decisions, it's as if they throw their stated values out the window and pull out a whole new set of values (operating values). Congruence has to do with alignment of values—you *do* what you *say*. If you don't, people won't trust you, and cynicism will reign.

- Establish the principles →
- Reduce these to behaviors ("by this we mean")→
- Select competencies based on the behaviors ("in short")→
- Note those competing behaviors that clash with the stated principle →
- Move the organization to align around the principles

Establish the principles. This first step of establishing the values cannot be perfunctory. What are the true core values, and are these the actual template that is used when decisions are made? Often we think about values to which we aspire, but don't currently employ. This can become a convenient escape hatch when it's obvious the organization is not living out its values. An organization may declare their core value is caring for people. Then they go about trampling on their employees in a mad pursuit of profit. Their core value isn't caring for people; it's making lots of money. That value determines how they make decisions. When and if this incongruence is noted, the leadership then declares, "Well, we aspire to care for people. It's just so hard to actually do it in the real world!" Remember, when the operating and core values are aligned, there is a high level of trust in the organization. When they are not, cynicism reigns!

Reduce values to behaviors. In this next step, we take the values that the organization espouses and begin to reduce these to specific behaviors. Okay, you care about people, so what does that look like? If I were to bring a video camera into your organization and begin to film, what activities would be recorded that show caring—something that is observable and measurable? Otherwise, we end up with these subjective, airy-fairy performance evaluations that are useless to everyone. When it comes to the value of caring for people, a behavior that supports this might be as follows: *each employee's opinions are taken seriously, it approaches people with an open mind and sensitivity toward the individual,* or *it pays attention in meetings rather than reads email.*

Note the competing behaviors that clash with the principle. We'll talk more about competing values when we discuss transformational leadership. For now, it is important to recognize that no matter what principle you establish as important to your organization, there will emerge competing behaviors that will pull you away from that stated principle. Recognizing these, admitting they are there, and then navigating them are critical to successful operation. Often the competing value is financial in nature. "If we actually employ this principle, we'll lose product value, or customers, or competitive advantage."

First, we look at the overview of our principles (usually cobbled together in a strategic planning session).

Our stated values (principles)

Principle	And by this we mean behavior(s) that readily supports this	In short . . .	Competing behaviors that clash with this principle
Flexibility	Demonstrates a willingness to work with alternative solutions, situations, and ideas	Shows balance between maintaining own opinions and considering other opinions	We have to adhere to a rigid schedule on certain projects, which excludes give and take

Collaboration	We are stronger as a team than as individuals. The best solution is with a team rather than a single mind	It's good to consider others but better to involve them. If you do it yourself, how do others grow?	I have to make a quick decision that doesn't allow the luxury of team involvement
Integrity	I do what I say and say what I mean. We are quick to acknowledge our mistakes. We give and receive feedback	Our actions are consistent with our beliefs.	Situations arise when I must act incongruently from what I have said
Innovation	We consistently seek to improve, to discover new ways of accomplishing our mission	We either grow or become irrelevant	The nature of our organization demands efficiency over innovation periodically

Next, we ask questions of each principle to see how it must be operationalized. This is critical to actually driving the principles down into the organization, so that they're not just slogans on the lobby wall, but actual lenses by which we monitor organizational behavior.

Principle	
Integrity	I do what I say and say what I mean. We are quick to acknowledge our mistakes. We give and receive feedback.
What does this look like in action?	<ul><li>Being prepared</li><li>Clearly communicating expectations and asking questions when expectations are unclear</li><li>Robust dialogue, open conflict, controversy accepted, voice of dissent being honored</li><li>Timely response</li><li>Others experience me living congruently with my values</li></ul>

How do we measure it?	• A 360 evaluation • Senior leadership team alignment • Following through on deliverables
What happens if we fail this principle?	• Authoritative management • Trust eroding or no trust • Withdrawals versus deposits with people • Instability and cynicism
What is the biggest obstacle to this principle?	• Saying what others may not want to hear • Unrealistic expectations • Pace, pressure, and time constraints • People's habits, personal feelings, and competing values
What are the key questions?	• What additional information do you need from me? • Do customers/peers believe in us? Do we believe in each other? • Are you putting yourself in the shoes of others? • Do I trust you? Am I treating others as I want to be treated?

Move the organization to align around the principles. The effective leader is one who is vigilant to the unfolding processes and behaviors within his organization, realizing that every activity within the organization is either forwarding the stated foundational principles or contradicting those same principles.[15] Unfortunately, most leaders become so entangled in the day-to-day operations of running their organizations that they are simply unaware of the slow drift so many organizations experience as the expedient overtakes the principled behaviors.

"I know it's important for our organization to act with integrity, but we'll go out of business if we aren't able to bring up the bottom line, any way possible."

---

[15] This is also true of each of us as individuals. Every act we perform is either confirming our stated values or contradicting them. We are either becoming more or less aligned and congruent as people.

Raising Up the Next Generation of Leadership

I devote the next to last chapter to this, but a word here is in order. We have said that the principles of an organization must be lived out daily within the organization in order for leadership to be trusted. Leaders must think long and hard about those who follow them. Does the next generation of leadership live out the values of this organization? If the answer is yes, the sustainability of that organization is much more likely.

The Battle

The battle that had begun purely by accident was now spreading as more units from both North and South were fed into the unfolding maelstrom. By midafternoon, Lee had cantered toward the battlefield to get a first-hand glimpse of what was unfolding and decide on next steps. His principal "eyes" that would give him the information he needed to make an informed decision, J. E. B. Stuart, was nowhere to be found. What to do? As he surveyed the situation, it appeared as though Heth's division, the first to engage that morning, was holding its own, while Ewell's whole corps was streaming down from points north and massing in just the right place to fall on the Union forces.

As the Union I Corps continued to fight stubbornly west of town along Seminary Ridge, the XI Corps under O. O. Howard marched up through town from the south and took positions to the right of the I Corps, facing north. Meanwhile, Meade was still far south of the fighting, unaware of the specifics of the unfolding drama that was slowly consuming more of his troops.

What is clear for both Lee and Meade is that they will have to trust their subordinates to conduct this battle in a manner that will bring success to their respective armies. And both generals are in a precarious position vis-à-vis their subordinates. Of Lee's three corps commanders, two have been in their position for less than two months, and neither has been in corps command before. Meade has been in command of the army for less than a week. He has no idea how his subordinates will function

under his leadership. But for now, neither general can worry about this.
Each must make quick decisions as to whether to continue this unfolding
struggle here at Gettysburg under these circumstances.

Take Action

- Think of a team you were on somewhere in your life that
  was successful. List the characteristics that made that team
  successful.
- Fill out the chart below.

Principle	By that we mean...	In short:

What does this look like in action?	
How do we measure it?	
What happens if we fail this principle?	
What is the biggest obstacle to this principle?	
What is the key question?	

Here are three questions to ask yourself concerning trust:

1. What am I doing to establish trust?
2. What am I doing to contribute to the distrust?
3. Is the lack of trust I feel a personal or a professional issue?
4. Have I done things to create feelings of distrust?
5. When I feel a lack of trust in someone, is there something
   I am doing to contribute to that?

Mutual respect, closely tied to mutual trust, respect is not readily given; rather, it is earned. One key difference between managers and leaders is that managers demand the respect they believe is due to them because of their title or position, whereas leaders know respect is earned through long-term consistent behavior. Mutual respect is crucial in complex and large organizations if for no other reason than one person cannot know or do it all. There should be a fundamental belief that we are in this thing together in collaboration. When addressing mutual respect issues, it is important to ask these questions:

1. What am I doing to garner the respect of those I work with?
2. What am I doing to garner the respect of those I work for?
3. What have I done in the past that would make people disrespect me?
4. What role do I think respect plays in my interactions with others?
5. How do I respect people who know more than I do at lower levels of the organization?

Chapter 3

How Should I Look at My Organization

How we see and understand our organizations is absolutely critical to our effective leadership of those organizations. To see and understand more accurately, often we need a "new pair of glasses" with which to see. In chapter 1, we talked about how critical self-awareness is. Now we will talk about organizational awareness and the critical nature of this perception.

The Battle

The first day of battle, July 1, was slowly drawing to a close as the sun began its descent in the west. Parts of two great armies had been shattered, beginning with northern cavalry and southern infantry accidentally colliding as the sun rose in the east. Confederate infantry had slowly driven back Federal forces toward the Lutheran seminary and the ridge that bore its name. Then the Union I Corps had arrived on the field and begun pushing back the southerners. And then, Ewell's II Corps had arrived at just the opportune moment in the precise place where they were needed, on the hapless Union right flank.

Howard's XI Corps had passed quickly north through Gettysburg streets and onto the fields to the right of beleaguered northern forces, only to find themselves besieged by more confederates streaming down from Oak Hill further northeast. Assailed from the west and north, the Union forces slowly gave way and began coursing back through the streets of Gettysburg and up onto Cemetery Hill just south of town, where the Evergreen Cemetery had received deceased townsfolk for just short of a decade. These two great armies had essentially crumbled into formless mobs after the day's fighting, victory being as disorganizing as defeat.

Commanders on both sides frantically attempted to sort out the various units and get men back to their principal regiments before the sun was completely gone. Men wandered about the battlefield looking for their units or for comrades who had fallen during the fighting. Wounded men cried out as they lay among the shattered accouterments of war. Field hospitals were hastily created in any available building. The surgeries would continue through the night and, indeed, throughout the coming weeks as the tally of wounded rose through the thousands.

But one thing was uppermost in the minds of those who were tasked with leadership: the army organizations had to immediately be sorted out and once again consolidated to face that maelstrom that would again consume them when the sun rose the next morning.

So how can we understand the nature of these two competing armies? How can we understand our own organizations? And why is it important to do so?

Arguably, the truly great leaders are those who are able to see their organizations as a whole, not just as disjointed departments. Having seen the organization as a whole, the leader can then muster the resources necessary and deploy them in the proper place at the right time. Likewise, in battle, the leader there not only understands his army as a whole, but sees the unfolding battle as a whole, not as a series of disjointed conflicts.

Whole-Brain Understandings

If there is one ability that is critical to effective leadership, it is the ability to see things differently (and in many ways, this book is about seeing things differently). Let's begin with how we see the world. Ways of seeing the world spring from ideas about how that world is organized. The history of ideas reveals not only the ideas themselves that have shaped the course of human history but the consequences of those ideas.

For three hundred years, the idea—the paradigm—of western culture has tended toward seeing man as machine, a thing to be taken apart and dissected, then put back together again. Comprehension of each component piece would lead to understanding the whole.

Then quantum physics came along and introduced a worldview where *relationship* is the key determiner of what is observed and of how particles manifest themselves. From this sprang the complexity of modern systems considerations that demanded new thought patterns. A system was understood as an entity with component parts that covary, with each part constrained by or dependent on the state of the other parts. System principles began to develop:

- Parts stand in some consistent relationship to one another.
- Parts interact with each other in a predictable, organized fashion.
- The elements, once combined, produce a whole that is greater than the sum of its parts.
- No system can be fully understood or explained once it has been broken down into its component parts.
- No element within the system can ever be understood in isolation since it never functions independently.
- Living systems cannot be directed down a linear path. Unforeseen consequences are inevitable. The challenge is to learn how to disturb them toward the desired outcome and then course-correct as the outcome unfolds.

As complex systems were observed and understood, it became impossible to find simple causes to problems, such as blaming individuals for organizational ills. All of a sudden, we were given a "new pair of glasses" by which to see the world. This is a pair of glasses that looks not just at the *what* of things (the content if you will), but the *way* things unfold and relate to one another—the process. And yet, people in the western world have not been very good at spotting processes. So let's look for a moment at how these processes work:

- All organizational processes are comparable—whether talking about a family, a government agency, a construction company, a medical practice, or a place of worship. Therefore, when considering an agency, a business, or what have you, the processes that are observed (leadership, change, communication, etc.) can be framed and dealt with in very similar ways.
- Systems tend to be broken—*the system is perfectly designed to give you the results that you're getting!* If you want to know what's going on, look at the pattern. In linear patterns, A's behavior causes B's behavior. In recursive patterns, A's behavior is in response to B's behavior, which in turn is in response to A's behavior. Determining whether A or B is responsible to the observed behavior is problematic and arbitrary.
- Systems maintain the status quo. In other words, the system is broken and tends to stay broken because change is so difficult and anxiety provoking to bring about, even when things aren't working properly.

In our own consulting practice, we devote our attention to the entire relational network system, not just the individual components—focusing on the connections and relationships between people rather than on isolated parts and problems within an organization. Again and again, we have seen that the health of an organization can only be assessed in the context of the whole. A change in one part affects to a greater or lesser degree every other part.

The organization regulates itself through feedback loops—outputs of a system are directed back as inputs, a chain of cause-and-effect that forms a circuit or loop. The system can then be said to *feed back* into itself. Information travels throughout the organization, giving it life, organic integrity, and stability. When that relational network malfunctions, the health of the entire organization is threatened.

The first day of battle was unfolding, with first Union cavalry engaging Confederate infantry in the fields west of town. As the day developed, Union infantry appears and engages more southern infantry, which is also hurrying to the scene of the fighting. Both northern and southern organizations are receiving information (input) while reacting to that information with particular behaviors (output) which is continually modifying the perceptions of what is occurring to the other side of the fight, and causing the behavior of individuals, units, and commanders to in turn be modified. Cause creating an effect, which itself becomes a cause, which in turn becomes an effect, etc.

Understanding the Whole

One critical issue that George Meade had to confront was the fact that three days before his elevation to the command of the whole Army of the Potomac, he had been only the commander of one seventh of that army, the V Corps. He certainly had some understanding of the other corps and how they cooperated together to make up the whole army (he'd joined the Army of the Potomac as a brigade commander during its fight the year before on the Peninsula). He'd served with a certain amount of distinction in his brigade (about 1500 men) and his corps (about 7000 men). But now he was responsible for an army of nearly 100,000. That's a lot of moving parts. And he would have to understand that army as a unit that would have to be carefully coordinated to engage and defeat the opposing organizational system—the Army of Northern Virginia.

You cannot sum up any organization by reciting the roster of its members. Every organization, from Disney and GM and Hewlett-Packard down to the real estate agency or church or retailer down the street, is made up of systems, patterns, traditions, attitudes, beliefs, and habits that—more than any *single* individual or *collection* of individuals—define and constitute that organization. Every organization has its own unique, collective personality, and that personality is always more than the sum of the individual personalities who inhabit that organization.

And yet, it is very difficult to step back (or get on the balcony, the preferred metaphor where the leader can remove himself from the fray and observe the unfolding processes creating the conundrum) to see the interaction of all the parts that together direct the behaviors of the individual components. This is especially true as problems begin to develop within organizations. Seeing a chronic relational problem as residing in *only* one person or *only* one department almost *always* misses the point. Problems in organizations grow out of complex patterns of interactions that involve most, if not all, of the people within the organization.

The person who is identified as "the problem" is usually the one who expresses the symptoms of the deeper systemic problem—and is often the one attempting to call attention to the real problem so that it can be solved. Tragically, these people are often punished as "troublemakers" when they are actually trying to save the organization from its own dysfunction. Unfortunately, most of us have a hard time recognizing the hidden, distorted, dysfunctional patterns in our relationships. We are too close to the problem to see our own enmeshment in the overall problem. And our minds have a way of covering up our own culpability in those problems.

So people try to sort out the situation by separating people into categories, looking for perpetrators and victims, good guys and bad guys, high-functioning departments and troubled departments. When we frame things in such stark terms, everything *seems* so much clearer. But it is *not* clearer. We have simply reduced our perception of reality to high-contrast black and white. We are not *viewing* reality. We are *filtering* reality—*and we may be filtering out the very information our organization needs in order to survive and prosper!*

The battle of Gettysburg is a good example of a complex systemic event that cannot easily be explained with simple, straightforward answers. Take, for instance, the notion of which leader won that battle? Which lost it? Was the winning or losing of the battle the result of any one leader? Or any leader for that matter? Any one unit?

Or combination of units? Which ones? There are no simple answers. Historians have wrestled with these questions ever since the firing stopped around that small town. For years following the battle, finger pointing became the norm for generals who had been at the battle. This was true in the South, where first J. E. B. Stuart, then James Longstreet were identified as the primary culprits. In the North, Dan Sickles tried for years to lay the blame for any Union failings with George Meade, while assuming all credit for the victory himself.

So What's the Real Problem?

As we've seen so many times in many organizations where we have been called to help, there is a full-blown crisis going on. People know that something is terribly wrong and needs to be changed—but what? Human nature being what it is, when something goes wrong, people immediately start looking for a scapegoat—someone or something on which to hang the blame. It might be an individual, a department, or a division within the organization. The thinking goes, "If only we could get rid of Jason . . .," or "If only we'd never hired Maureen . . .," or "If marketing would only pull its weight . . .," or "If we could just spin off the overseas division, everything would be fine!" So we give Jason and Maureen the axe, we rattle the cages over in marketing, and everything is solved, right? Wrong. Things get *worse*. The "solution" doesn't solve the problem—the "solution" *becomes* the problem.

When my consulting company, TAG, is engaging a new client, we rarely, if ever, accept the problem as stated by the client, not because we think the client is lying, but because people usually have such limited understanding (a faulty pair of glasses) of relational systems of which they are a part. Whenever there is a problem in any group of people, whether that group is a family or an organization, there are often two problems: (1) the identified problem and (2) what we like to call "the thing in the bushes." The identified problem is what people *think* is wrong. When someone asks, "What's wrong here?" everyone points to the identified problem. Sometimes the identified problem is the real problem, and it can be solved with a simple technical fix (we'll discuss this more fully in chapter 5).

More often than not, however, the identified problem is unspoken—giving it even more power and influence. But when we try to solve a problem, and we keep getting stuck, then the identified problem is *rarely* the real problem. In such cases, the *real* problem is what we like to call the thing in the bushes (we'll discuss this as the adaptive or transformational problem in chapter 5)—and that's the problem nobody even sees, much less talks about. That's because invariably the people telling us the problem are *part* of the problem—a factor they have failed to notice. When I used to counsel families, parents would bring me their problem children with the entreaty, "Please fix my child!" What was not said was, "Oh, by the way, don't change me. Just leave me the way I am!"

When we assume that the identified problem is the main barrier to reaching our goals as an organization, our tendency is to apply inadequate or misplaced solutions that never address the reality of the situation. And if you only treat a symptom, you may relieve the pain for a time—but you'll miss the cancer at the root of the pain.

Whole-Brain Problem-Solving

Let's look a little deeper at these concepts. We have shifted in recent decades from Newtonian to quantum ways of seeing the world. This has led our culture to place more emphasis on left brain activity—information processing, the communication of verbal or textual content, mathematics, logical reasoning, science, engineering, technology, and so forth. Rational, symbolic ideas that can be expressed in words have been favored in our culture over the intuitive, the imaginative, the emotional, and the relational. The left side of the brain—which is the dominant side for most people—is the brain hemisphere of which we are most aware. It operates out in the open, in ways that we consciously recognize. Books and e-mail messages are written, speeches are delivered, mathematical expressions are formulated, ships and airplanes are constructed, cities are built, and missiles and space shuttles are guided by the left side of the brain. The right side of the brain tends to work in the shadow of the left, gathering and processing its information underneath the level of human awareness.

The graph below compares the operations of the left and right hemispheres of the brain:

Left side (aware)	Right side (unaware)
Verbal	*Spatial*
I hear what you say.	I see what you're doing.
Intellectual	*Intuitive*
That argument makes perfect sense.	My hunch says this won't work.
Analysis	*Synthesis*
Let's pull this problem apart.	Let's fit the pieces together.
Directed	*Free*
Let's follow the agenda.	Let's let our minds roam free.
Objective	*Subjective*
Let's base our judgment on the data.	I've just got a feeling about this.
Realistic	*Impulsive*
Let's conduct ourselves in an orderly way.	Throw caution to the wind.
Rational	*Metaphorical*
Give me the facts.	Tell me a story.
The individual	*The relationship*
It's all his fault.	We should share the blame.

Only lately has there been a shift in focus from left brain activity to right brain activity, from the parts to the whole, from single-channel verbal content to multichannel verbal-visual-emotional content, from individual actions to relational networks. We are discovering that, in organizations, interactions between people are rarely isolated and simple. Rather, interactions are complex and connected in a weblike network of relationships with others in the organization.

Let's consider this new "pair of glasses" for looking at problems from a different perspective:

1. Learn to focus on the whole, not just the parts.

Relational systems thinking looks at the forest not just the individual trees, or in the metaphor we'll use later; it gets on the balcony to peer down on the dance floor noting the intricate interactions. Systems thinking looks at the organization as a complex whole, not a simple collection of parts. You cannot understand an organization merely by listing the characteristics of its individual members. In addition to those individual characteristics, there are complex dynamics at work, such as *synergy* (the interaction of two or more individuals so that their combined effect is greater than the sum of their individual abilities), *chemistry* (the way different personalities and capabilities interact and enhance each other), *rapport* (the ability of individuals to harmonize and get along), and *morale* (optimism, confidence, and esprit de corps).

In his book *Ahead of the Game*, Pat Williams, the former general manager of the Philadelphia 76ers observes from his own experience that a basketball team is much more than just a collection of talented stars. In fact, during the 76ers' glory days, when the team was anchored by the legendary Julius "Dr. J" Erving, Pat Williams discovered that a team can actually be *less* than the sum of its parts! He explains:

> We opened the 1976–1977 season with a home game against the San Antonio Spurs. Dr.

J led the charge, closely followed by a whole roster of marquee names: George McGinnis, Doug Collins, Darryl Dawkins, Lloyd Free, Caldwell Jones, and Joe Bryant—a team that the sports reporters instantly dubbed "the best team money can buy." Amazingly, however, the best team money could buy went out and lost its first two games.

Coach Gene Shue and I sat down and talked about the disappointing start of the season. We decided that our win column was empty because our roster was too full. We didn't have a basketball team—we had a flying circus! We had too much talent—everybody wanted twenty shots a night. We had Lloyd Free proclaiming himself the prince of midair. Darryl Dawkins, adopting a moniker that could not be topped, proclaimed himself all-universe. Joe Bryant and Steve Mix continually elbowed each other for more court time—and the chemistry between Dr. J and George McGinnis was always touchy.

We moved quickly to correct the situation, trading a couple players, putting a couple more on the injured reserve list, and waiving a few others. Once we had pared the team back, Gene Shue was able to get this expensive collection of talented egos under control—and the 76ers began winning games. After a 0-2 pratfall start, we went on to win 50 out of 82 games.

That's the way it is in any organization. A successful team is more than a collection of individual talents. In fact, a team consisting of moderately talented individuals working in sync, with strong synergy, chemistry, rapport, and morale, will usually beat a more highly talented "flying circus" of prima donnas and inflated egos. In a healthy organization, where relational systems thinking is practiced rather than linear, simplistic thinking, the whole truly is greater than the sum of the parts. Coach Mike Krzyzewski took over the men's national basketball team for the 2008 Olympics. The '04 team had been made up of NBA stars, who were promptly beaten in that Olympics. Coach K, after taking over, selected lesser talents who could function as a team. The result was two gold medals in the next two Olympics.

The game of billiards is very simple if you only have two balls on the table, a cue ball and a billiard ball. Hit the cue ball at the billiard ball, and with a good aim, you can predict with great precision where the billiard ball will go. It's a matter of simple geometry. But if you have an entire rack full of billiard balls on the table, the game becomes much more complex and unpredictable. The path of any given ball—say, the seven-ball—becomes completely unpredictable, because it is enmeshed in a network of relationships with all the other moving balls on the table. During a single shot, the seven-ball's path will be jostled and deflected numerous times by contact with other balls. Where will the seven-ball end up? Impossible to predict. The seven-ball is one individual component in a complex network of dynamic relationships.

Those relationships become even more complex when you are dealing with thinking, feeling, living beings instead of unfeeling billiard balls. Newton's third law of motion says that for every action, there is an equal and opposite reaction. So, according to Newton, if you kick a ball, you will get an equal and opposite reaction from the ball. By transferring a certain amount of kinetic energy to the ball, you will send it flying in a fairly predictable way.

But when dealing with living beings, we need to know more than Newton's third law. If you kick a dog or a person, you cannot expect the same reaction you would get from kicking a ball. The dog might run and cower—or it might come after you and sink its teeth into you. If you kick a person, he might run away, kick you back, have you arrested, or sue you. Living beings and living networks are much more complex and unpredictable than linear, Newtonian arrangements of dead matter.

People are complex. The network of relationships within an organizational system is complex. Relationships among people in organizations are constantly changing, rearranging, and evolving. A change in any one member affects other members and the group as a whole. A change in the group as a whole affects each individual member. Every action is also a reaction. Individual members affect the organization; the organization affects individual members.

These ping-ponging, zig-zagging, fluid, dynamic effects make it difficult to separate cause from effect—and these effects make it difficult to assess blame when things go wrong. The question "Whose fault is it?" becomes extremely complex. It's not as simple a matter as "Bill yelled at Jack, so it's all Bill's fault." Often, as we begin to untangle all the various interwoven causes and all the many interrelated effects, we find that Bill yelled at Jack because Jack ignored Bill's request; because Nanci does not feel confident in exercising authority over Bill; because Hank, the editor-in-chief, has not set healthy boundaries within the organization; and the board of directors has not established clear leadership parameters, all of which has generated a widespread mood of distrust throughout the organization, and on and on and on!

The point is not that we should excuse individuals and the poor choices individuals often make. There must be individual accountability within organizations. But at the same time, we need to broaden our thinking so that we can begin to grasp the complex relational dynamics that play out among people in organizations. When problems arise that threaten the overall effectiveness of organizations, the cause of those problems is usually found not in a specific individual, but in the relational system of that organization.

Contrast the performance of Dan Sickles, commander of the Union III Corps, and Winfield Hancock, commander of the Union II Corps, who was lining up next to Sickles as Meade was extending his line south down Cemetery Ridge. Sickles could only see his III Corps position and judged that it was inadequate, so he pulled it out of line and moved it forward three fourths of a mile. He did not take into account the effect on the whole Union army lining up north of him.

Winfield Hancock, as we will see in Part II, understood much more clearly what the whole picture was on the south side of the Union line, indeed, the whole Union line, as Longstreet would launch his flank attack, pitching directly into Sickles' overextended corps. For several hours, Hancock shifted and re-shifted Federal units to meet impending disasters as each developed along the southern line. Hancock saw much more of the whole picture. Sickles was myopic.

Linear versus recursive patterns. Let's return to the Newtonian way of seeing things. The old Newtonian way of seeing things was linear. One person acted upon another. "You made me mad." "We didn't make our third quarter goals because John didn't work hard enough." When a consultant hears a person or multiple persons explain a problem, almost invariably linear designations are employed. "My coworker made me late to the meeting." Or, "Robert E. Lee lost the battle of Gettysburg."

Linear

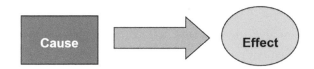

The new systems way of seeing the world brought in a recursive sense of cause and effect. In recursive ways of understanding, there is feedback, each part affecting the other. The old "You made me late" became "You were late because I was mad and treated you like an imbecile, which only made you later (because that was your best chance to get back at me) which only made me madder, which only made you later, and on and on."

Recursive

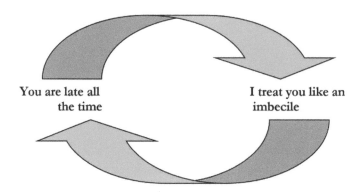

You are late all
the time

I treat you like an
imbecile

This recursive pattern makes it impossible to tease out cause and effect so easily. One cause is also an effect. The pattern is self-perpetuating.

Relational systems thinking is focused directly on such issues. Old style linear thinking—the kind of thinking that is commonly employed in most organizations—is incapable of even detecting such issues. The real causes of a problem would not even show up on the radar screen of a linear thinker. The solution to most major organizational problems can only be found in the whole—-not in the discrete parts.

2.   Learn to focus on relationships, not just individuals.

As we have seen, the old, ineffective way of assessing problems in organizations focused on individuals in isolation. The more accurate way of understanding problems in organizations requires us to look at relationships, at the way people relate to one another, not just at separate individuals.

At TAG, we have developed an exercise we call "relational network mapping." We begin the exercise by having people in the group identify the top six or seven specific problems affecting the organization. They frequently identify such problems as poor communication, conflict, lack of trust, confusion over values, and so forth. They may even identify a specific person as the problem. We write these different problems on a flip chart and circle each one, placing each problem in its own little bubble. That is how the group views the problems in the organization—each one in its own isolated bubble.

But then we ask them to draw lines of cause and effect between the bubbles. "Well," someone says, "I can see that poor communication leads to lack of trust . . ." So we draw a line between those two bubbles—"And lack of trust leads to conflict . . ." and "Oh, and confusion over values leads to conflict, too"—two more lines and on and on, more and more lines connecting more and more bubbles. It quickly becomes apparent that what seemed to be a lot of isolated problems are actually connected by lines of cause and effect—lots and lots of lines, an uncounted number of lines.

And the group begins to realize that the bubbles aren't the problem and the people aren't the problem. The *lines* are the problem. And what are those lines? *Relationships*! And the entire group experiences an astounding breakthrough in understanding. They realize that you never find the thing in the bushes hiding in one of those bubbles, in the identified problems. It hides in the hidden space between the bubbles—in the relationships between the problems. This insight transforms our understanding of how to effectively solve relational problems in organizations.

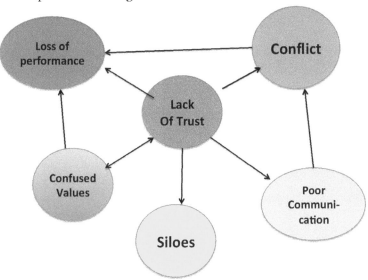

In an organization, the web of relationships is everything. Being aware of the relationships in the organization means being continually aware of all the factors that affect those relationships—factors we explore in detail in other chapters of this book (such as communication, boundaries, and trust).

People in relationships are constantly communicating. Communication is the glue that holds relationships together—and when we talk about communication, of course, we mean *all* communication channels, both verbal and nonverbal. Relational systems thinkers don't just focus on the verbal content, the "what" of communication. Relational systems thinkers also focus on the "how" of communication, the nonverbal, emotional, and relational elements of the communication process. Even the most subtle behavioral cues are recognized as important channels of communication. And because of the multichanneled nature of communication, the ability to get my thought across to you clearly and accurately becomes more difficult than first imagined.

Take another look at the conflict between Bill and Jack, two principals in an organization. During the time Bill had worked with Jack, he and Jack had continually been at each other's throats. They had developed a set, predictable pattern of communication. As a result, the patterns of communication and behavior among other coworkers were affected. People knew they had to avoid talking about Jack to Bill, just as they had to avoid the subject of Bill around Jack. Whenever Bill came into the office, some people (especially those who were uncomfortable around conflict) found some excuse to leave the office. At the same time, others (those who tended to be placaters and peacemakers) would try to distract one or both of the combatants and prevent them from coming into contact with each other. The conflict between Jack and Bill impacted the entire office in a variety of negative ways, distorting the routine, the behavior, and the communication patterns within the entire organization.

The problem in the above organization was much bigger than a struggle between two individuals. It was a dysfunctional dynamic that affected the entire relational system. The problem could only be solved by looking at *all* the affected relationships—not just the individuals involved.

3.   Understand that organizations seek to maintain organizational balance (homeostasis), which is often unhealthy.

People naturally tend to avoid change—even healthy change. Organizations, being made up of people, are no different. They avoid change. They seek to maintain a steady, stable state—even if that stability is unhealthy and painful.

Question: how is your golf swing? If you are at all like the author of this book, chances are you've got some bad golfing habits. Problem is, after performing a bad swing for a long enough time, doing it *wrong* begins to feel *right*. We easily become comfortable with an ineffective swing. Go take lessons with a pro, and you'll find that the pro is telling you to do some things with your golf swing that feel wrong and unnatural. You'd much rather stick to what feels comfortable—even though it causes you to slice like crazy. That's normal. That's human. But it's also self-defeating.

The same is true of organizations. Because relational networks seek balance, predictable patterns tend to emerge, becoming repetitive, redundant, and counterproductive. We saw these patterns in Bill and Jack's organization. In fact, it wasn't just a pattern. It was a *game*.

Bill would come into Jack's office, strut around and talk about his awards, and demand that Jack change his work product. Jack, resentful of Bill's demands, would find ways to sabotage, camouflage, and obscure all the best elements of Bill's work. At that point, one of the admin assistants would invariably rush in to find out what all the shouting was about. She'd try to get both sides to "make nice." This little game—this *pattern*—took place several times a week. It wasn't a disruption of the routine. It *was* the routine—but nobody seemed to realize it.

These patterns of interaction within organizations go largely undetected because people rarely "get on the balcony" to see the big picture. Instead, people tend to focus on the details, the individuals, the issues of the moment, little realizing that the issues themselves are unimportant—mere minutiae. The *real* issue, the *bigger* issue, can only be found in the behavioral pattern.

Patterns of behavior and communication in relationships operate underground, beneath the level of our awareness. They are subtly constructed and elaborately maintained. Any attempt to change them is unconsciously but strongly resisted. Once we become consciously aware of the enormous influence of these patterns on the organization, we can make the changes and adjustments that produce a relationally healthy organization.

    4.   Learn to set appropriate boundaries.

As we saw in the previous chapter, healthy boundaries fence off the relational systems of the organization from the outside world and also mark off the subnetworks within the organization. Healthy boundaries give form to healthy relationships, which in turn lead to healthy boundaries. Those boundaries should neither be too rigid nor too lax.

As we assessed the problems in Bill and Jack's organization, we found that a lack of healthy boundaries contributed to the destructive conflict in the office. They both allowed their personal, emotional agendas to invade the workplace. Instead of acting professionally for the good of the magazine, both became embroiled in personal, emotional turf battles. Professionalism went right out the window.

The admin's attempts to jump in and mediate the disputes between Bill and Jack were yet another violation of boundaries. She could have explained to each of them the impact their behavior had on her, but she should not have gotten in the middle of their disputes.

When TAG came in to make an assessment, our consultants saw that the entire relational system was unwittingly maintaining an atmosphere of conflict and sibling-like rivalries which were slowly sucking the life out of the organization. We helped the leadership "get on the balcony" to see the unhealthy relational processes that were unfolding, how the system as it now functioned was defeating all of the best efforts of individual performers. As leadership grasped this, they began to make much needed changes.

The Battle

The first day of battle was nearly over. Confederates had fought disjointedly in the morning and early afternoon. But in the later afternoon, they are able to coordinate better their attacks, and they had prevailed. Northern troops, who had been routed and driven through Gettysburg, entrenched up on Cemetery Hill alongside the division Gen. Howard had judiciously left in reserve up on the hill before deploying the other two divisions north of town, where they were overwhelmed and beaten. As the shadows of evening extended across the landscape, Union gunners placed cannon among tombstones in the town cemetery, preparing to defend the hill when morning light broke across the countryside.

Because Meade would not arrive on the battlefield until near midnight, command had been passed from senior commander to more senior commander as the day has worn on—first Buford, then Reynolds (killed), then Doubleday, then Howard, then Hancock and Howard, then Slocum.

In surveying the situation toward late afternoon, Lee could now see that Cemetery Hill was quite possibly the key to the entire Union position. If that hill were strongly occupied by Union forces, they would be very difficult to dislodge in the coming days. It is also the perfect artillery platform, able to sight guns in all directions. Lee sent a message via courier to Gen. Ewell: "Take that hill, if practicable." There was the rub—if practicable meant discretion on Ewell's part.

Some have surmised that if Stonewall Jackson had been on the scene (he'd died a few weeks earlier having been shot accidentally by his own men at Chancellorsville), he would have scrambled up the hill and secured the place in a flash. This assessment fails to take into account the daunting nature of the task Ewell (leading Stonewall's old corps) faced. His men were exhausted and disorganized, victory being as disordering as defeat. Because a whole division of Federal troops had been stationed on the hill, there was already a substantial defensive position established. True, shattered Union forces had been streaming up onto the hill during the late afternoon, but Howard and later Hancock were quickly organizing them as the belated XII Corps also arrived and went into position. Added to this was the false report that possibly fresh Union troops had been spotted north of the town. At any rate, it is rather cavalier to say that the hill could have been easily taken. Much of this thinking points to remnants of Lee's thinking, and thus a central part of that southern army code, that Confederate troops were invincible, and a successful attack could easily have been organized and prosecuted in the late hours of the first day.

Within the minds of all who had fought that first day, thinking and attitudes as to what had happened were already taking shape—thinking and attitudes that would mold subsequent behavior of each army organization. This in turn would shape the history and legacy of those organizations and indeed the nation. Heroes and villains were already emerging. Myths to explain these recent events were already being recited around thousands of campfires that dotted the landscape in and around Gettysburg.

The first day was now at an end. The two armies would fight one of the most horrific battles the nation has experienced on the second day of battle.

Take Action: Seeing the Whole Organization

- List several of your organization's or family's distinguishing norms (e.g., my organization is very hierarchical; my family never eats meals together). What is their impact on your group's ability to deal with challenges? (e.g., Communication only flows in one direction, i.e., up the hierarchy. Because we don't eat together, our family rarely has dedicated time to talk about what's important and how to handle challenges.)
- What behaviors are considered inappropriate in your organization? Yelling? Heated debate? Casual attire? Long

lunches? Long weekends? Leaving at five o'clock instead of later? What do these rules suggest about your group's code and its adaptability?

- What behaviors do your organization's compensation and recognition systems encourage? Discourage? How well do the encouraged behaviors support the organization's strategic goals?

- What does your company's organization chart say about which functions and roles are valued most? Valued least? Looking at who has direct access to whom, what might this imply about who is designed to work together and who in isolation?

- Ask each member of your team to write a brief, anonymous story about an incident or event in the organization that they think reveals the enterprise's values.

Part II

The Second Day

The first day (July 1) at Gettysburg had been an accidental stumbling into one another of two great armies. Neither commander had wished to fight at this time in this place. But circumstances had conspired against them, and as more and more units on both sides approached the town and surrounding fields, they found themselves swept into a maelstrom that grew in intensity as the day wore on.

The end of that first bloody day found both armies exhausted and somewhat disorganized. The Confederates had "won" that first day, but victory can be as unsettling and disorganizing as losing. The leadership on both sides was tasked with sorting out the various units, getting men back to their regiments and into line, determining the characteristics of the terrain, and aligning forces for the struggle which would undoubtedly unfold the next day.

O. O. Howard's XI Corps had been routed coming to the aid of Reynolds' I Corps (Reynolds having been killed) when Ewell's Confederates had swooped down on the XI by accident in the exact right place. Howard had wisely left one of his three divisions in reserve on the hill that was quite possibly the tactical key to the whole subsequent Union position. Now as the shattered remnants of his other two divisions, along with the decimated I Corps, made their way through the town and up onto this hill—Cemetery Hill—and mounted their cannon among the tombstones of Evergreen Cemetery, Howard, who was soon joined by W. S. Hancock, began to align his men for the next onslaught.

Meanwhile, Lee was trying to sort out the two corps—A. P. Hill's III and R. S. Ewell's II—that had shattered the Union lines that afternoon (Longstreet's I Corps was in the rear of march and had not yet reached the battlefield). Men in butternut were scattered through the town and over the fields to the north and west of Gettysburg. Cemetery Hill was the key to the whole field, but with darkness fast approaching and Lee's men disorganized and exhausted, could a successful attack be mounted now, or would this have to wait till morning? Ewell decided not to attack. Lee had to content himself with deciding what would be his next move on the morrow.

Even though serious fighting this day would not begin until four o'clock in the afternoon, the ferocity of the fighting as these two armies tore one another apart would leave many thousands dead and wounded—the second day in itself ranks as the tenth bloodiest battle of the Civil War—with far more casualties than the much larger Battle of Fredericksburg the year before.

This day would see the necessity of proper alignment with the organizations, the accurate understanding of leadership demands depending on certain variables, and the effective handling of conflict within the organizations.

Chapter 4

Alignment: How to Align the Self-Interest of All Participants with the Mission of the Organization

Alignment can be seen as bringing the people within an organization into line—*the proper adjustment of the components for coordinated functioning.* We align the efforts, energies, and strategies of our organizations around a common direction, operating culture and business approach that supports success.

The Battle

It was not yet dawn on July 2 when Lee sent out several scouts to investigate the Union lines, in particular, to ascertain how far to the south toward the Round Tops the Federal line extended. It is still a mystery to history as to where these scouts actually went and what they then saw as they groped around in the darkness south of Gettysburg. But they returned to Lee stating that they had been up on Little Round Top (that is basically an impossibility, given that they would have undoubtedly run into Union signalmen). They went on to state that the bulk of the Federal troops were up on Cemetery Hill over a mile north of the Round Tops, with a short tail extending down Cemetery Ridge toward the Round Tops, but nowhere near that area in any force.

Lee at once saw opportunity. Ewell still faced Cemetery Hill and Culp's Hill, both of which at his own discretion he had decided not to assault the evening before. A. P. Hill had his corps from the left of Ewell around the town to the west extending a little south. Longstreet was now coming up (he had not participated in the first day's fighting), and his corps would be perfect for use against the Union left. If Longstreet could sneak his corps down below the spine of Seminary Ridge and get into position south of the Union lines, he could sweep up Emmitsburg Pike and smash into Federal forces before they were able to bring up the rest of their army and extend down to the Round Tops—a workable plan in theory. Unfortunately, the intelligence the scouts had brought to Lee was inaccurate. Yankees were already extending down to the Round Tops, and their position was quite formidable. Longstreet couldn't proceed on this flanking mission as proposed. He'd have to revise and improvise as he got into position later in the day and saw what the actual situation was.

Confederate commanders needed to be apprised of the situation. Lee determined that Ewell would feign an attack (not a full-scale attack, but a "pretend" attack if you will that gives the enemy the idea that you are attacking there) in the Culp's and Cemetery Hill area. Then Longstreet would sweep up from the south along Emmitsburg Road slamming into the Federal flank on and near Cemetery Hill.

Now all that was needed was for the commanders, then the troops, to be aligned with this plan, and everyone sent off to do his part of the mission. There were only two problems. First, the Union troops weren't where they were supposed to be. Second, the principal commander, i.e., Longstreet, didn't agree with the plan. Longstreet understood the overall plan of battle, as the Confederates crossed into enemy territory, would be for southern forces to get into a strong defensive position and invite the Union army to attack them. No one, to Longstreet's thinking, had said anything about Confederate forces attacking. He argued for southern forces to disengage from Gettysburg, swing south and set up a strong position between the Union army and Washington and wait for Federal forces to attack. But Lee was adamant, and the plan was set in motion.

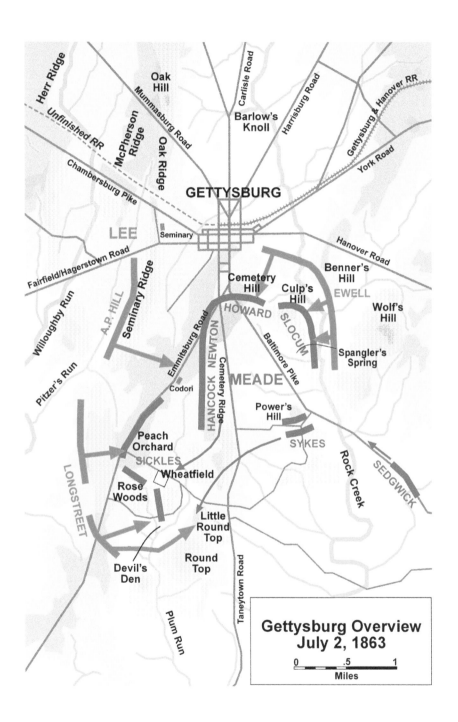

**Gettysburg Overview
July 2, 1863**

0   .5   1

Miles

General Meade had arrived at Gettysburg late in the evening of the first day. He was apprised of the situation and immediately began shifting troops and feeding arriving units into his lines, extending his position from Culp's Hill and Cemetery Hill south down the ridge that extended from the cemetery toward the Round Tops that jutted up a couple of miles to the south.

From the start, Lee's second day plan went awry. Ewell didn't attack when he was supposed to. Longstreet had to backtrack while getting his corps into position on the flank of the Union army due to the faulty intelligence. And there is evidence he was slow because he had not "bought into" the plan. And when Longstreet finally got into position late in the afternoon of day two, Federal forces clearly were not where they were supposed to be, and plans had to be significantly revised.

On the Union side of the line, as the sun came up on the second day of battle, there were also problems with alignment. General Sickles had decided he didn't like the place where he had been positioned—aligned with the rest of the Union army—and had pulled his men out of alignment and moved forward (see the map above). This lack of alignment put the whole army in extreme jeopardy. In a competitive environment, be it sports or warfare, lack of alignment and its attendant gaps are exactly what opponents will exploit. It is the place of greatest vulnerability.

Once you are on the journey toward self-awareness and clear definition as a leader (and therefore internally aligned and aligned with the mission of your organization), you are able to establish trust among your subordinates. And then once you've come to terms with the culture of your organization, and how that needs to be shaped and preserved, you're ready to align the organization around the mission.

A word of caution, be aware if you are not self-aware. (And if so, you will undoubtedly be unable to spot this fact. Others who know you well will have to make you aware of this.) This lack of self-awareness usually leads to internal misalignment (what you say is not what you do). This then compromises your ability to build trust and align your organization. There is absolutely no way around this fact.

What Is Alignment?

Alignment, as we said, brings the people within an organization into line—*the proper adjustment of the components for coordinated functioning.* We align the efforts, energies, and strategies of our organizations around a common direction, operating culture and business approach that supports success. The rule of thumb is this: the more alignment you have across individual, departmental, and organizational goals, the more purposeful execution you can expect. Without consistent alignment, there is little chance for successful implementation of any plan.

Alignment is a leading indicator of the speed of growth of a company. This is particularly true if you consider not just alignment between the executive team or alignment between the executive team and the employee base, but alignment between the shareholder or stakeholder motivations, alignment between what we say is most important with what our organization is actually trying to accomplish (and therefore investing resources in those initiatives). The things that are most important are also the things we have the most people working on, which are in turn aligned with the customer demand, what's actually happening in the marketplace.

We'll start with the fundamentals. There are some basics to developing aligned organizational culture that can't be ignored.[16]

Organizational alignment focuses on several areas—processes, people, and systems—bringing them into alignment with each other. Organizations struggle when any one of these elements is out of alignment.

The Army of Northern Virginia is a prime example of an organization with dedicated leaders, excellent soldiers, and a clear mission that could not maintain alignment during the battle. As a result, they lost the battle. Union forces also had serious problems with alignment on the first day (Barlow pulls out of line for better ground) and the second day (Sickles pulls out of line for better ground). Both incidents seriously compromised Union alignment.

---

[16]   These concepts are expanded in *Secret Sauce* by Ford and Osterhaus.

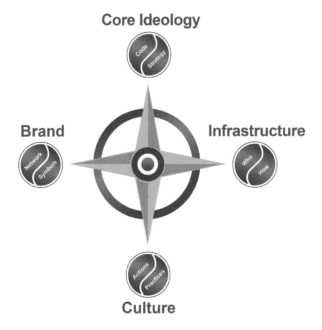

The above diagram indicates the component parts of core alignment.

These components are critical no matter whether one is talking about an army, a government agency, a multinational corporation, a club, or a family. Let's take a look at each one:

Core ideology. An organization's core ideology consists of two components, code and strategy.

Code. A healthy, productive and successful organization is built upon a clear guiding code, which is the essence or DNA of every organization. The code is comprised of the organization's culture, values, mission, vision, and goals.

The code sets the direction for all the members of the organization. It is the group's lodestar or compass point. The code keeps everyone in the "boat" rowing in sync and in the same direction.

When the code is clearly understood and every member buys into it, allying himself or herself with that code, then the entire organization pulls together. When a few people lack commitment to the code—either because they don't grasp it or because they actively disagree with it—you have people rowing out of sync and in the wrong direction. Before long, the "boat" is going around in circles instead of moving forward.

If the code is the organizational life force, the heartbeat of everything that occurs in and around the organization, then it shapes the face an organization displays to itself and the world. It should answer these questions:

- Our identity: Who are we?
- Our tradition: Who are our heroes (people who embody the essence of the organization) and how did we get here?
- Our values: What do we believe in?
- Our mission: What do we do and why are we here?
- Our vision: Where are we going?
- Our strategy: How will we get there?
- Our rituals, symbols, and style: How do we reflect our code? Collective activities that have become engrained in the organization.
- Myths: key stories (which may actually be true) that illuminate moments in the organization's history that were turning points. What are the stories we tell about ourselves over and over again?
- Visuals: the architecture, furnishings, landscaping, logos, graphics, etc. that are the outer face of the organization to the world. What is the "look" of our organization?

Apart from the similarities in the two armies at Gettysburg, there were marked differences in the codes of these two armies. The Army of Northern Virginia was truly ragtag. When marching into Frederick, Maryland, during the first invasion of the North in the late summer of 1862, people remarked that they could smell the army long before it came into view. People spoke of the most disheveled collection of scarecrows they had ever seen. They were, of course, a rebel army, and as such, their attire matched this moniker. They traveled light and fast—Stonewall Jackson's units were known as foot cavalry. They pitched into battle with an ungodly caterwauling that tended to unhinge their oppo-

nents. *This howling, wailing, squealing, shrieking cacophony became known as the rebel yell.*

Over against this was the Army of the Potomac. They were much more of a spit and polish organization that, on the surface, looked much more professional than their counterparts. George McClellan had put his indelible stamp on them, a stamp that would last through much of the war. He had instilled a pride in them, though he had not been able to aptly lead them on a battlefield. McClellan and his lieutenants were cautious, carefully engaging opponents only reluctantly or when surprised and forced to clash. This army contained more ethnic characteristics, one of the most prominent being the Irish Brigade which fought themselves practically into oblivion at Antietam and again at Gettysburg.

And of course, there were the two differing ideas as to why men had signed up to join each of these two armies. In the North, men had signed up with the idea of preserving the Union, a nation that was worth saving. The southern secession was a rebellion that needed to be suppressed in order that the Union that had been established eighty-five years previously would continue.[17]

Southerners, on the other hand, in many cases saw their move to secede as similar to the founding fathers, led by George Washington, breaking away from an overbearing North that was threatening their very lives and livelihoods. And of course there was slavery. Though few southern soldiers owned slaves, the institution was imbedded in the southern culture, and to threaten it was to threaten the southern way of life. The states had come together years before voluntarily, to form the Union. States could just the same leave the Union voluntarily.

Now consider strategy:

Strategy. Strategy can be seen as the intentional allocation of resources—resource allocation to fulfill your mission—realizing that your context is ever-changing. The organization differentiates itself from competitors, all the while adding benefit to its custom-

---

[17] Slavery, for the most part, was not seen by most enlistees as the reason for the war.

ers. Limited resources demand prioritization, an essential aspect of strategy.

Think again of the Army of Northern Virginia. Lee comes under most criticism around this issue of strategy. His strategy tended to focus on Virginia, and its security, and on the one set piece battle that would crush a Union army, win recognition by European powers, and grant southern independence (Lee understood that the South could not win a protracted war of attrition).[18] Because of the priority of the eastern theater, a disproportionate amount of resources was allocated to the eastern war theater in general, Virginia in particular.

Obviously, an effective strategy is essential to the surviving and thriving of the enterprise. Many experts have considered Lee's strategy— the one set piece battle in the East that effectively destroys a Union army and thus wins recognition for the South—as a poor strategy (and in light of the final outcome, they may be right).

Infrastructure. Infrastructure as the second dimension of core alignment asks both the **who** and the **how** question of the organization.

Who. The *who* of your organization is not just the people who populate your organization. It is the talents that each of your people possesses that is the true focus. Successful people understand their talents and strengths *and build their lives upon them.* Successful organizations don't just accommodate the different talents in their people; they *capitalize* on these.

As we begin to think about aligning our people, it is important to think in terms of the talents that each person within the organization brings to the table. Unfortunately, too many leaders are intimidated by a diversity of talent around them. They are much more comfortable with clones of themselves. It is also much easier to align, when all talents are similar. That might be good for alignment, but is awful for the diversity of talent needed to execute the mission of the organization. And it can easily lead to group think. Effective teams

---

[18]   Most civil war battles were inconclusive, and though one army usually yielded the field, the ability to declare a complete victory was usually absent.

need diversity of talents which must be understood, properly utilized, and aligned with one another.

My colleagues Ken Tucker, Shane Roberson, and Todd Hahn write about prevailing talent at length in their book *Your Intentional Difference: One Word Changes Everything.* A person's intentional difference (ID) is defined as the spontaneous, observable, reliable, and measurable patterns of thinking, feeling, and behaving. Cobbling together high-functioning teams involves several critical steps:

1. Identifying the specific behaviors that will be needed to successfully complete the mission.
2. Reducing these specific behaviors to talents.
3. Identifying people possessing those talents to include on the team. Some of this is intuitive. But there are measures to identify talents as well, well-known ones such as Myers-Briggs Type Indicator©, the DISC©, and Clifton StrengthsFinder©.
4. Aligning (and continuing to align) the team around the mission.

How. The *how* involves the structures and processes within the organization. An organizational structure defines how activities—basic management, task assignment, and coordination between departments—are directed toward the achievement of organizational aims. A process is a collection of related, structured activities or tasks that produce a specific service or product (serve a particular goal). An organization can be structured in many different ways, depending on its objectives. The structure of an organization will determine the processes in which it operates and performs.

Unfortunately, what is often the case, the structures and processes that were useful in defining yesterday's organizational problems and activities are still in place today. And more often than not, today's organization demands a whole different set of structures and processes. At these times, yesterday's answers become today's problems. But unfortunately, the status quo will always work against the forces for change (to be discussed further in chapter 7).

Alignment is maintained as the structures and processes are continually evaluated to ensure that they are serving the needs of the organization *as these exist today.*

Culture. Culture is the third dimension that is considered in core alignment. You can't change code, but you can change culture. Remember what we said about code—it is the over-arching DNA of the organization that must be understood in order to develop a healthy culture. Code to an organization is what talent is to an individual—it's the hardwired essence of that individual. For an individual, a talent doesn't turn into a strength until practiced repeatedly. Likewise, code doesn't turn into a positive culture until recognized and nurtured.

Culture is reflected in two areas: the practices and the actions of the organization.

Practices. Practices are those actions that we intentionally perform, in each organization "what we do around here." These practices involve everything from when employees show up for work, to the rituals performed with each potential customer in a retail setting.

Actions. Actions are the unintentional behaviors which most often are performed outside of our awareness. Because they are outside of awareness, we do not consider these, and they can lead us toward incongruence and mistrust. A CEO talks about inclusiveness, and yet he spends practically no time with women or minorities, creating a "white men's club" in the C suite. This is precisely why it is absolutely critical for the leader to be self-aware—to capture those inadvertent behaviors that may in fact fly in the face of stated values.

More often than not, practices lead to actions, especially when there is alignment with the other elements we have discussed—the well-defined leader leads an organization that contains a healthy code and strategy, with an infrastructure populated by people who are in the "right seats," exercising their talents to forward the core ideology, which is clear to them.

In the last chapter, we talked about Lee and Meade being aligned with their respective governments and national regions. All leadership within an organization must be aligned with the culture, beginning with the mission, vision, and values of their organizations. If not, there are only two options: change the culture and bring it into alignment with the leader or leave.

Now, as we think about alignment, we need to consider the aligned leader who is tasked with bringing into alignment the organization—each member of that organization being aligned with the mission of that particular organization.

Alignment and the big arrow. So we've established that organizations need to become and stay aligned. The question now arises: around what do we align? One metaphor I like considers the organization as one big arrow that contains lots of little arrows—projects, businesses, clients, and business deals. The big arrow is your organization's code, including mission, strategic direction, core competencies, and core values. The leader and his leadership team own that big arrow. And it is around this big arrow that alignment must unfold. The problem is that, often, the little arrows begin to point in different directions as people solidify their silos, bicker among themselves, default to self-interest, and neglect the larger mission. And in the process, the whole organizational alignment begins to crumble. Senior leaders have the responsibility to make decisions and act in ways that break through silos and align everyone with the strategic and cultural direction of the company. That's how they can ensure all the arrows will be shooting in the same direction.

Remember what we said earlier. Successful organizations are guided by a compelling code. And this is also how they align:

> Our identity: Who are we?
> Our tradition: Who are our heroes and how did we get here?
> Our values: What do we believe in?
> Our mission: What do we do and why are we here?

Our vision: Where are we going?

Our strategy: How will we get there?

Our rituals, symbols, and style: How do we reflect our code?

To sum up, alignment involves bringing meaningful purpose, practical strategies, and goals together making an organization's aspirations more credible—and more likely to be achieved.

Another way to understand alignment is the willingness to sacrifice self-interest for the sake of the organization. Effective leaders have the ability to channel the self-interest of employees into the organization's interest, aligning them around the mission. And this is exactly where a compelling, meaningful code is most useful.

What Creates Alignment?

Crisis. As we have already mentioned, crisis immediately creates alignment. It's easy to align people in crises—when individual interest melts away and organizational interest is paramount. But how do you create that same kind of alignment in the absence of a crisis? We'll also see below that often, even in extreme crisis, it's hard to maintain alignment.

Compelling code. In the absence of crisis, there must be another element that draws people into alignment—and that element is a compelling code. A healthy organization is built upon a clear guiding code (the essence or soul of that organization). It is crucial that the people in an organization be committed to the code, as the code sets the direction for all the members of the organization. It is the group's lodestar or compass point or gyroscope. The code keeps everyone in the "boat" rowing in sync and in the same direction—aligned. When the code is clear and every member buys into it, allying himself or herself with that code, then the entire organization pulls together. When a few people lack commitment to the code—either because they don't grasp it or because they actively disagree with it—you have people rowing out of sync and in the wrong direction.

Meade not only had a crisis that assisted in bringing about alignment; it is arguable he had a compelling code. For most in his army, the mission in that code was to preserve the Union and not allow southern states to walk away and essentially destroy the republic. Six months earlier, Lincoln had also issued his Emancipation Proclamation freeing slaves in rebellious territories (this was a war time executive order that would have to be hammered into law toward the end of the war). This second piece of the Union code was met with a mixed reception, some troops heartily embracing it and others rejecting it as an initiative they could not accept. But whatever the opinions of individual soldiers on that evening of July 2 concerning freeing slaves, they now prepared their cooking fires and stared across fields littered with the dead and dying, heard the screams of comrades, and knew that they had to stay in place and aligned because of the necessities of the moment. The crisis trumped all other considerations.

When the third day of battle dawned (July 3), Lee placed Longstreet, the man who was in disagreement and misaligned with Lee's tactical plan, in charge of the southern assault on the Union center on Cemetery Ridge. Historians disagree as to whether Longstreet's beliefs about the battle plan interfered with his ability to prosecute what he deemed to be a disastrously flawed plan (later known as Pickett's Charge). Needless to say, when a principal subordinate, tasked with carrying out an initiative, strenuously objects to that initiative, there is undoubtedly going to be problems with the proper execution of that initiative.

To create alignment, you must constantly evaluate your processes and structures to ensure that you are preserving your code and updating your strategy. The status quo is tenacious. In organizations, as in golf, poor posture and a weak grip don't typically happen overnight. Bad habits have a nasty habit of creeping in over time. Organizations that were once aligned can drift out of alignment, with disastrous results.

Maintaining alignment. What makes maintaining alignment in any organization so difficult is that it's an ongoing process. It's not a one-time adjustment. As conditions change, as personnel change, as strategies change, alignment must be constantly monitored, and modifications made.

The status quo and alignment. All organizations fight to preserve the status quo, even if that results in death! Because of past successes, many leaders put their processes on "cruise control" and don't attend to that which will allow them to maintain their momentum through alignment.

Short-term decisions and alignment. Short-term decisions are by nature tactical. They are meant to resolve the immediate crisis while restoring order in the moment. However, there are two significant problems when constantly using this approach. First, over time, short-term solutions begin to conflict with other short-term solutions creating confusion, conflict, and misalignment in the ranks. Second, short-term solutions fail to address underlying issues that create chronic long-term problems.

At the battle of Gettysburg, Lee and Meade employed short-term decision-making to constantly adjust and readjust their lines and plans of attack and defense to meet the presenting danger and opportunity. Troops were borrowed from one sector to shore up another.

Lee's planned flank attack on the second day led by Longstreet against the Union left was just such a situation. Lee ordered Longstreet to launch a surprise attack with two divisions straddling, and guiding on, the Emmitsburg Road. The objective was to strike the Union army in an oblique attack (en echelon), rolling up their left flank, collapsing the line of Union corps onto each other, and seizing Cemetery Hill. Unfortunately, the plan was based on faulty intelligence because of the absence of J. E. B. Stuart and his cavalry, leaving Lee with an incomplete understanding of the position of his enemy. The plan would have been good if in fact the Union left flank was "in the air" (unsupported by any natural barrier) as an early morning scouting expedition seemed to indicate. In reality, by dawn of July 2, the Union line stretched the length of Cemetery Ridge and anchored at the foot of the imposing Little Round Top. Lee would have to quickly alter his plans.

Meade would have to employ the same short-term decision-making. On the afternoon of the second day, Meade thought his lines were completely aligned running from Cemetery Hill down the ridgeline to Little Round Top to the south. This had been the case that morning, as both armies anticipated the other's next move. Dan Sickles, the political general with a mind of his own, had decided independently to reposition his III Corps to what he considered a more advantageous position almost a mile forward from the aligned Union lines. When Longstreet began his late afternoon attack, both Lee and Meade were surprised by what they found. Lee found the Union army greatly extended beyond what he had been led to believe. Meade found his line now misaligned with a whole corps at the end of the line completely out of position.

As evening approached on the second day and the sound of battle rose to a deafening roar to the south of town, both Lee and Meade had to rethink their earlier plans according to the developing situation. For Meade (and especially General Hancock who was in overall charge of this southern section of the battlefield), units had to be quickly redirected to the points where they were most needed to shore up crumbling lines. Lee, on the other side of the line, was attempting to understand the unfolding situation and feed troops into a whole new plan that had emerged, more by happenstance than by design. Union lines had extended much farther than he had anticipated, and his initial musings and planning would no longer be applicable.

Over time, as long-term problems remain unaddressed because of short-term decisions that continually emerge, the credibility and competency of leadership are questioned by employees at every level, further increasing stress and tension in the system. And the first casualty in that stress and tension is the alignment of the organization.

The Battle

As George Meade was attempting to align his various corps that were coming onto the fields south of Gettysburg as the sun was mercifully setting on that first day of battle, he was attempting to understand the lay of the land and the best troops he had on hand to defend certain portions of the field. Dan Sickles was bringing up the III Corps, and the problem for Meade was what to do with him. Meade tucked him way down at the end of the line, instructing him to stretch his corps to touch the Round Tops. Meade thought that the brunt of the southern attack would fall on Cemetery Hill.

Having Sickles, the consummate narcissistic and inept political general, now placed well out of harm's way was the best course of action.

What Sickles proceeded to do was take his men out of alignment with the rest of the Union army and move three fourths of a mile up onto what he deemed to be a better placement (in the Chancellorsville battle two months before he'd been ordered off a hill that was an excellent artillery position and had seen his men torn up as a result).

Actually, General Sickles is following the lack of alignment model that Francis Barlow set on the first day of battle (July 1). Barlow, a minister's son, is the ultimate Brahmin —graduating first in his Harvard class, close ties to the intellectual circles of Transcendentalists, a lawyer in New York. He has been promoted for his bravery and commitment, but he is disliked by his men, who find him a hopeless martinet. His disdain for the largely German-born soldiers he leads is thinly veiled.

On the first day of battle, Barlow dutifully led his division (under O. O. Howard) through the town and out into the fields north of town where Howard places him to the right of Carl Schurz. He carefully deploys his men as directed, then spots what he considered to be a more advantageous position (just like Sickles) on Blocher's Hill (now Barlow's Hill). The position proved too far forward from Schurz's division, forming a dangerous salient. Onrushing Confederates under J. B. Gordon overwhelmed the position and Barlow was taken from the field by Gordon's men severely wounded. Even in the midst of extreme crisis, Barlow and Sickles both defaulted to self-interest—"This position is better for me, therefore I will assume this position, and the rest of the army will have to adjust and align accordingly." Both of these self-interested blunders nearly cost the Union the battle (and could have quite possibly led to the downfall of our nation).

Lee looked at the battlefield at Gettysburg and thought he saw a similar scenario as Chancellorsville, where he had succeeded marvelously. He had hit both flanks, then sent a force up the middle to win the battle. Unfortunately he did not take into account the various factors that had changed—two new corps commanders (Jackson wasn't there), a new Union commander, a different topography and alignment of the Army of the Potomac, etc.

And by the way, leaders don't themselves answer all the questions that are posed to them. That's the old definition of leadership: the leader has the answers—the vision—and everything else is a sales job to persuade people to sign up for it. Leaders certainly provide direction. But that often means posing well-structured questions, rather than offering definitive answers. Imagine the differences in behavior between leaders who operate with the idea that "leadership means influencing the organization to follow the leader's vision" and those who operate with the idea that "leadership means influencing the organization to face its problems and to live into its opportunities." That second idea—mobilizing people to tackle tough challenges—is what defines the new job of the leader.

Lee had his fictions that he stubbornly believed: we're invincible. I can do the exact same thing with new corps commanders (A. P. Hill and Dick Ewell) that I've always done with James Longstreet and Stonewall Jackson, i.e., give them an overall plan of battle, and then have them execute it as they see fit.

Meade had his own self-deceptions: I can safely place Dan Sickles away at the end of the line, and he won't be able to cause anyone any trouble. And, if I just ask my subordinates what might be the best course of action, they'll come up with my conclusions, and I'll be able to do what I had planned and later plead that it wasn't my decision alone.

On the evening of the second day of battle (July 2), Meade called his principal leadership team together seeking consensus on what to do the following day. He realized that he had only been in command a few days (having risen from the status of a peer to overall command). Obviously he had a crisis on his hands. Several of his seven corps had been decimated in the previous two-day fighting. Longstreet's attack on the left flank the afternoon of the second day of battle had come within a hair of being successful.

Meade, as he gathered his leadership team in the house of the Widow Leister, had to decide whether to hold his ground where he now stood, attack Lee's army, or withdraw to what might prove to be a safer place. He took a vote, and the majority voted to stay in place on the defensive.

Lee, contrary to Meade's evening meeting with his direct reports, didn't call his leadership team together. He evidently took counsel princi-

pally within himself as to what to do on the third day. His principal general, Longstreet, was in total disagreement with him as to what should be the next course of action. Longstreet wanted to abandon any attempt to get at Union troops at what he perceived as an impregnable position and swing around behind the Federal army and get a more favorable position. Quite possibly Lee, the consummate conflict avoider, didn't hold a council of war precisely because he didn't want to deal with Longstreet and the pushback he would offer. It is unclear if A. P. Hill and Richard Ewell, Lee's other two corps commanders, voiced any particular opinion as to how to go forward with the battle. It is unclear as to whether Lee even consulted them at all as to next steps.

Take Action to Bring About Alignment

The following are crucial questions:

- Do you and your staff and employees have a common understanding of your organization's core purpose?
- Does your spending match your priorities? Are you putting your money where your mouth is?
- Do your priorities match the needs of your constituents?
- Are all of the various departments and people aligned for successful achievement of the plan, or are there situations where key goals are at odds?
- Are people told to do one thing, but rewarded for the opposite?
- Are there systems, processes, and policies in place that are in direct conflict with achieving key goals?
- Does the plan call for bold risk-taking, yet the culture in the organization is completely risk averse?

Chapter 5

The Leadership Triangle

Tactical, strategic, transformational considerations. When it comes to leadership, organizational functioning confronts the leader with many different issues that must be addressed—tackled in differing ways—wearing different leadership "hats" if you will. Unfortunately, leaders often approach every issue wearing the same hat, with the same posture and procedures, procedures that have worked in the past in different contexts. But contexts change, and what worked in a past context may not necessarily work in the situation now facing the leader.

The Battle

The second day of the battle, as the afternoon drew toward a close, James Longstreet launched an epic attack on the Union left. Having formed his corps in the woods and behind the swales to the south of the Union lines, he flung his juggernaut at the Federal line. His attack was to be en echelon, a rolling attack that would first hit Little Round Top, then Devil's Den, then the Wheat Field, and finally Mr. Sherfy's Peach Orchard along Emmitsburg Pike. The attack would prove relentless and ferocious. It would come dangerously close to succeeding. Lee was betting the attack's tactical success on the skill of his commanders, the invincibility of his warriors, and surprise.

What had brought these two great armies to face one another in this tactical standoff that would determine the trajectory of our nation going forward? In many ways, this particular tactical battle can be seen bookended on one extremity by strategic thinking and planning that had determined the allocation of the limited resources of the South brought to bear on the North in an attempt to force independence. On the other, extremity was the transformational speech of Abraham Lincoln that would place not only the battle, but the whole struggle in context for the American people, defining for all Americans going forward, the nature of our republic.

Strategically, Robert E. Lee had moved his army out of Northern Virginia into Maryland heading for Pennsylvania for the second time in less than a year in the summer of 1863. The political, social, military, and environmental situation in the South had been shifting, and Lee and President Davis had divined a strategic plan that to them would be the most advantageous to the health and ongoing viability of the southern Confederacy. War needed to be visited upon the northern people so that they could share in its horrors and begin to petition the government for its conclusion. A decisive battle needed to be fought in which the Union army was essentially destroyed and foreign powers could understand the strength and legitimacy of this newly created nation in the South.

While the commandant of West Point, Lee had read extensively on Napoleon and his campaigns. One fact had apparently jumped out at him. Napoleon contended that it was not a good idea to protect one's capital directly when engaging an enemy. It was more advantageous to proactively maneuver incessantly, not allowing your own army to be driven back to the capital. Evidently President Davis and General Joe Johnston had missed this vital lesson when they were at West Point, for both had seen the protection of Richmond as paramount as they devised their strategy for engaging the Union army in the fall of 1861 and spring of 1862.

But Johnston was wounded in the suburbs of Richmond defending the capital, and Lee took command. He began with slashing attacks on the Union army. Then for the next two years, he put Napoleon's ideas into practice, maneuvering around the Union army up into Northern Virginia, then into Maryland in the late summer of 1862. Now it was mid-summer in 1863, and Lee had again crossed into northern territory, employing his strategy of maneuver away from his own capital.

As Lee entered Cashtown, Pennsylvania, on the morning of July 1 and heard the ominous sound of cannon off to the east signaling a fight, he quickly had to remove his strategic hat and don his tactical hat and direct the most horrific battle ever fought in America.

On the other side of the line, George Meade was also in the process of discarding the strategic hat (I must protect Washington while locating and engaging the rebel army) for the tactical hat. Fighting had broken out west of the little hamlet of Gettysburg. Elements of his army had been routed and driven through the town, but evidently had assumed an excellent defensive position.

And now the crescendo of battle rose louder and louder on this fateful second day of battle. Union defenders, from the 20th Maine and its heroic professor-commander, Joshua Chamberlain, who helped save Little Round Top and the Union left; to Col. William Colvill and the men of the 1st Minnesota, who were sacrificed to gain fifteen minutes to bring in fresh troops on Cemetery Ridge; to Pap Greene, whose ingenuity and resolve saved Culp's Hill and the Union right, struggled as the sun slowly ebbed in the west. The fighting was desperate and, at times, nearly hand to hand. Casualties mounted rapidly. And everywhere on the southern half of the field, Winfield Hancock rode furiously about, spotting holes in his line, and filling each, just in the nick of time.

We have seen that the effective leader is the one who is well defined and self-aware, thus able to be congruent and internally aligned. He, being congruent, is able to build trust. And he is able not only to understand the organization as a whole and protect the culture of the organization but also to align that organization for effective operation. Now, it becomes important for this well-defined leader to understand the several activities of leadership and how differing situations demand differing stances in leadership.

The Leadership Triangle

At the core of leadership is our belief that different kinds of leadership challenges call for different types of leadership options, choices, and postures the leader must assume. The most pressing leadership question of the moment is not just about profits or growth or shareholder value or market share. It is this: what does it mean to lead in such a way that my team or organization can adapt, compete, and thrive? This is the case whether you are leading a family, a business, a department, a volunteer board, an army, or a faith-based committee.

We understand that there are three primary types of leadership challenges, represented by the three sides of the triangle. Each challenge requires a different mode of leadership behavior in response, a different option. Most leaders fail to identify the type of problem and therefore fall back on their preferred, or default, option. The art of leadership is in knowing what sort of problem you are facing and what leadership option is required to tackle it. Each problem requires a different set of skills, language, questions, and styles of interaction.

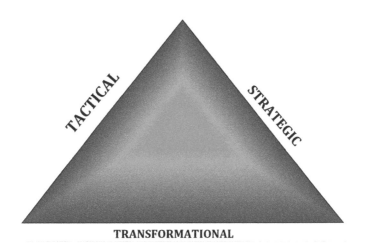

TRANSFORMATIONAL

As you understand the principles of the leadership triangle, you'll see that the same leader often behaves very differently depending on the nature of the problem he confronts. Glance at the chart (adapted from *Governance as Leadership* by Richard Chait et al.). This summarizes some of these differences based on whether the challenge at hand is technical (tactical), strategic, or transformational (transformational).

	Tactical	Strategic	Transformational
Role	Expert	Synthesizer	Facilitator
Tone	Confident	Vision casting	Creative
Key question	What's wrong?	What's the focus?	What's the question?
Problems are to be . . .	Solved	Planned	Reframed
Interaction	Training	Inspiring	Free-flowing and robust
Tense	Present	Future	Past, present, future

In our work with hundreds of organizations, we've observed that successful leaders use three primary modes of leadership: tactical, strategic, and transformational. Let us explain.

Tactical problems. Tactical problems and decisions are those decisions on a battlefield that determine how armies will engage one another in combat. *We can look at how Generals Lee and Meade and their subordinates acted and reacted on the three days of July 1863 as the battle of Gettysburg unfolded. Military units were brought to the scene, deployed, and rearranged depending on the exigencies of the unfolding struggle.*

When the problem is technical (tactical), the leader's role is that of an expert or an expert finder. His tone is confident—"we can apply our current base of knowledge to solve this." The key question he raises is, "What's wrong here?" and the evident problems are to be solved. As he interacts with his people, he functions as a trainer, authority figure if you will, bringing knowledge to bear. And he functions in the present tense—"how can we solve this problem right away so that our today can be better?"

Tactical problems are solved by experts. If the roof leaks, hire a roofer. If your computer network is down, call the Geek Squad. If you break your leg, get an orthopedist. Most leaders function in this mode most of the time. Leaders have risen to the top of their organizations precisely because of their expertise in handling the various situations that have confronted their companies. So with their subject matter expert (SME) hat firmly in place, they go about directing the organization forward.

Leadership teams bring their own expertise to the table: financial, technological, managerial, and so forth. If the organization is considering a new building project or capital campaign, it is appropriate for others to bring their expertise to the table. To solve a tactical problem, simply find a person who has the expertise and authorize that person to solve the problem. Tactical leaders exercise their will through their expertise.

Lee has been considered a tactical genius in many ways, and this is born out in his creation and execution of battle plans. But he, as are many authority figures, was hampered by his seeming inability in certain situations, to exercise and enforce his will upon subordinates. Many have argued that he was much too courteous and conflict avoidant (discussed later in this book) when subordinates pushed back on what he knew to be what was needed.

This was most apparent with General Longstreet, who routinely pushed back on Lee's expressed wishes (often expressed as a wish and, to Longstreet, a suggestion, rather than a direct order). At the battle of Second Manassas (Bull Run), Stonewall Jackson's command was under heavy assault, and Longstreet had drawn his corps into position to Jackson's right, in perfect position to assault the Federal left. For most of a day during that battle, Lee suggested attack and Longstreet demurred, preferring to wait until conditions were more advantageous. The day ended with no attack from Longstreet. He did attack the next day and drove the Federal army from the field. But many have argued that if he had attacked the day before, when Lee thought it best, the Union army might have been destroyed.

Jackson, on the other hand, tended to intuitively sense exactly what Lee wanted, and all Jackson needed was the suggestion, and he swung into action according to Lee's intentions. Lee attempted to handle Longstreet the way he handled Jackson. But the two men were wired quite differently. Longstreet demanded direct orders. Jackson could take indirect suggestions and put these into play aligned with Lee's intentions.

Generally, people are promoted and placed in positions of authority because they demonstrate technical expertise in their area of interest. They get results in the work they do and they are recognized for that expertise.

Once in authority, it behooves the individual to identify his scope of authority. In every role that people play—professional, personal, or civic life—there is a scope of both formal and informal authority. People are authorized to perform in certain ways by formal authorizers (usually those above you in the hierarchy). This scope is probably explicitly laid out in a job description, in rules and regulations, or in organizational bylaws and organization charts. Part of what makes knowing your scope of authority difficult is that the limits of your authority are typically opaque and always changing. That is even true for your formal authority, your job description, or what you were told at your hiring conference. Have you ever been hired into a job, told what you were supposed to do, and then when you started to do it, run into a brick wall and learned what was in your real but unwritten job description? Often, in our experience, people are hired as change agents and quickly come to realize that the person who hired them was part of the problem, but that changing that person was not in the job description. In fact, as you attempt to make changes, this person becomes the biggest barrier to change, though he said in the interview that is exactly what he wanted.

If a situation arises within your scope of authority, but you don't handle it well, your scope shrinks. Every time you have a situation arise within scope, either you handle it well and increase the scope, or handle it poorly and decrease the scope.

The Functions of Authority

There are three major functions or services of authority:

1. Direction
2. Order
3. Protection

Direction: As you would suspect, this has to do with clarifying the future for the workforce, communicating repeatedly where we are going, what we are trying to achieve, what my role is in achieving the goal, and how we will measure our progress over time. This is a leadership task—*define the future for the workforce.*

Order: This is the process of creating the norms and customs that determine how we behave around here, how we settle differences between people or groups, and how we treat people. Norms and customs are part of the culture and always exist. The only questions are as follows: Are they created by leadership or by default? Are they intentionally designed or are they designed by circumstances? Often there is gradual decline and in some cases loss of positive norms in the workforce as a whole. This is one of those transformational issues—a *silent threat* that increases risk in the system.

Protection: This is about exposing the workforce, at a rate they can tolerate, to the internal and external threats that potentially could undermine both the long-term well-being of the organization and the long-term well-being of the workforce. Protection at first may sound like a paradoxical concept. Here, the idea is exposing the workforce to the challenges they are going to face in the near future so they have time to adjust and make the necessary changes needed to deal with what is coming their way. If in the traditional sense of "protection" we shield them from threats, we are effectively preventing them from getting prepared to cope with the inevitable.

Longstreet's late day attack on the second day was complicated, with many moving parts that needed overall coordination from an authority figure. But this figure was apparently conspicuously absent as the battle unfolded. Two of Longstreet's divisions (Hood and McLaws) would lead the attack. Longstreet was clear about this. But then Richard Anderson would take up this rolling attack after Longstreet's divisions had done their work. But Anderson was part of A. P. Hill's corps, not Longstreet's. So who was to direct him? Hill seemed to think he had turned that responsibility over to Longstreet. Longstreet evidently assumed Hill maintained control. A Lee staffer said later that "the whole affair was disjointed." And Lee, the overall commander, how did he perform that afternoon? His orders were slim to none, and those issued were indistinct. Even then, the South came dangerously close to succeeding in their assault.

Strategic Challenges

When the problem is strategic, the leader's role is that of a synthesizer, bringing together knowledge of the internal organization, the external constituency, and the broader climate. His tone is that of casting vision, introducing an inspiring picture of the future that takes advantage of and confronts the changing landscape. His key question is, "What should be our focus?" and he realizes that the key way to tackle problems is through innovation and integration. His interaction with his followers is best described as inspirational and he focuses on the future tense—the imagined and aspired to results of careful adherence to a clearly articulated strategy.

Jefferson Davis' strategy involved maintaining the integrity of the new nation against northern invasion around the enormous perimeter of the South. This required not only stationing troops at key points across the borders but bringing to bear large armies at key points for defense when northern threat loomed.[19] But soon this strategy was deemed impractical, and an offensive-defensive strategy was employed. Unimportant southern areas would be ignored as troops were concentrated to meet Union armies where they appeared. Southern offensive strikes would be mounted when opportunity presented itself. This strategy was immediately embraced by

---

[19]   This was indeed a gargantuan task given the enormous size of the South.

Lee and led to the South's two invasions of the North, the first in the late summer of 1862 and the second in 1863 that ended at Gettysburg.

It is in this strategic arena that Lee received his most vehement censure from military historians. Being the principal military advisor to President Davis at the beginning of the war, and already having had a lifetime of military service, Lee arguably was in the best position to synthesize the existing military elements in both northern and southern armies to make informed decisions as to strategic direction. He noted in 1862 that the South was apparently beginning to lose, especially in the western theater, and what was called for was a dramatic reversal involving a large set piece battle that would at once dishearten the northern people's will to fight and bring European powers in on the side of the South.[20]

Strategic challenges relate to external changes. They are future oriented. They are about major transitions. Such challenges require more than a tactical fix. Strategic challenges require strategic leadership, the art of leveraging strengths in order to minimize weaknesses and capitalize on opportunities. But strategic leadership often involves dealing with opposition, as internal stakeholders may resist the needed change. Strategic leaders are on a quest to understand their external environment. They must ask big-picture questions:

- How do people think?
- What motivates people?
- What do they value?
- How do they form relationships?
- How do they make decisions?

Strategic challenges have to do with responding to the world outside your organization. These challenges are not necessarily problems to be solved, but challenges you can anticipate. Strategy has to do with

---

[20] Many have also argued that Lee's sustained focus on Virginia as the principal site for resource allocation and operations hobbled the Confederacy's ability to wage a successful struggle for their independence.

surveying the environment outside your department or organization and deciding how best your team can adapt to external opportunities and obstacles.

Strategy is a systematic method of differentiation from the competition. It is based on priority activities, performed in unique ways, reinforced by current practices, to produce a distinct result. Everything about strategy is unique. That's why United Airlines could never reproduce Southwest Airlines strategy. Nor could McDonalds ever replicate Subway's strategy. They are in similar industries, but strategy is all about differentiation. And once something becomes commonplace (like dollar menus) in a certain context, it is no longer strategic. Everything about strategy is rooted in context.

In the face of strategic challenges, tactical effectiveness is not enough. Anyone can operate effectively and still go out of business, fail in a charitable fund-raising endeavor, or coach a losing team. Strategy is when you choose a unique value proposition through a series of activities that become rooted in your system. Essentially, strategy is what differentiates your organization from any other.

Strategic challenges require a different, and in some ways more sophisticated, set of skills than tactical problems. But strategic acumen does not cover every type of leadership challenge. Often, when strategic direction is established, the result is that a whole different set of issues surface, issues related to values, behaviors, and attitudes.

Strategic decisions involve the overview of how a war will be conducted in light of the unfolding sociopolitical climate, what priorities will be given to what initiatives, etc. *In addition to the constant use of maneuver, Lee's overall strategic considerations centered on one thing in his mind: the need for the one set piece battle in which the southern forces would substantially destroy a Union army, thus gaining recognition (and its attendant legitimacy) to the Confederacy. He knew that the South could not win a protracted war. He also did not consider the western theater of the conflict to be worthy of substantial resource allocation. In addition, as mentioned, because he was first and foremost a Virginian (the priority that allowed him to walk away from his American citizenship), he never was able to shake the idea that his pri-*

mary strategic focus should have been on the entire Confederacy, not just Virginia. He was not alone in this. As the war unfolded, southern governors constantly howled for more troops to be sent to their states, leaving President Davis to consider the Confederacy as a whole as best he could.

Transformational Issues

When the problem is transformational, the leader's role is that of a facilitator, inviting dialogue and discovery, particularly in the areas of values and beliefs. The tone he strikes is one of creativity—whether in problem-solving or in conflict! He knows that the key question now is itself, "What's the question?" and that problems are not so much to be solved or planned for as much as navigated and reframed—considered in an entirely new way. He knows that group interaction at this level of leadership needs to be free-flowing and robust—everything on the table—and that his focus is not only on the present but also on the past and the future. Transformational challenges are the very stuff of leadership and require a leader operating at full creative capacity.

An issue requiring transformational change is much more complex and is sometimes hidden within the systems and structures of the organization. We are seldom aware of transformational issues. They mostly revolve around competing values. This is why strategic direction often surfaces transformational issues. The new direction challenges the status quo.

Transformational issues are often hard to identify clearly, require changing hearts and minds, and often are championed by someone who cares but may not have the authority to effect change. When transformational issues are involved, people have to learn new ways and must choose among what appear to be contradictory values. Technical or tactical issues can be *managed*. Transformational issues require leadership to resolve them—hence the name transformational leadership.

Transformational leadership is difficult work, difficult because it involves helping individuals make hard value choices and difficult because it challenges what people hold dear and thereby generates resistance from many of those affected. When people resist transformational work, their first goal is to preserve what they have, and that means shutting down those advocating leading the change.

Transformational issues always bring competing values to the fore. They aren't easy decisions. Transformational issues require different skills than tactical problems, especially the ability to manage and occasionally even orchestrate conflict. Very few people in positions of leadership have developed these skills. The transformational side of the triangle will be discussed in depth in the next chapter.

In the last chapter, we will see transformational issues that faced Lincoln and Lee. For Lincoln, it was the competing values of equality versus economic stability maintained by slavery. For Lee the competing values also revolved around slavery—maintaining the institution during a protracted war versus freeing and arming slaves to help in the southern cause.

Leadership would be a safe undertaking if organizations and communities only faced problems for which they already knew the solutions. But most problems come wrapped up in transformational *and* tactical aspects. The easiest way to avoid the transformational issues is to focus on the technical aspects. But when this is done, the transformational has a habit of emerging and distracting the whole process of decision-making and change.

True transformational leadership is dangerous. That's because the leader engages people at the deepest levels of their personhood, a level where people often do not venture. And, that leader is often pointing out things that people do not wish to face. Almost invariably, this involves the fact that they are often at odds with themselves within themselves—competing values actually haunt every individual and every organization.

Let's take a look at an example. An employee who is handicapped with significant physical limitations is on a highly technical team. He comes to his supervisor:

"I feel that the people on my team don't respect me."

"How so?" asked the supervisor.

"They ignore me and give me only menial tasks to perform."

"I'll talk to your team." The supervisor lines up the team and chews them out for not including the limited employee more effectively (a technical solution).

"We can't use him effectively," a team member protested. "He slows the whole process down. We have strict deadlines, and to exceed these creates multiple problems."

"Yes, but," the supervisor stammers, "we are mandated to include this person meaningfully in our work. So we have to integrate him on the teams."

"Perhaps," another team member piped up. "So how do we do that, and not compromise our work?"

Note the competing values in this transformational issue: doing quality work (value #1) versus assisting a handicapped employee to get integrated into the team (value #2). These competing values often show up for leaders who wish to empower employees. Empowering employees often competes with the value of high-quality performance. In other words, if I empower you, I can't control the quality of your work as closely as I can control my own. So I'm reluctant to let you be empowered because of the competing value.

There are all manner of competing values when one thinks about it:

- Securing sufficient resources and additional personnel support to thrive (rather than survive) in my job *versus* avoiding conflict at all costs to maintain the precious harmony we now enjoy by not approaching and upsetting those who control the purse strings
- Sticking closely to the beliefs and principles our organization was founded upon *versus* compromising in small, surgical ways to increase the bottom line
- Promoting the most qualified candidate *versus* being loyal to a good friend who could use the promotion and its attendant pay raise
- Quality *versus* quantity

- Efficiency *versus* innovation
- Preservation *versus* change
- Protection *versus* challenge
- Consistency versus variety
- Expansion *versus* preservation
- Transparency *versus* confidentiality
- Standing on principle *versus* compromising
- Commonality *versus* difference
- Individual considerations *versus* community considerations

The list is endless. What makes competing values so difficult is the fact that it's not a good value trumped by a bad value. Both values are valid and useful. They just happen to compete with one another. To embrace one is to contradict the other. This is why the stakeholders themselves must do the primary work of wrestling through the implications of the competing values, the leader facilitating the conversation by first pointing out what the competing values are, then monitoring the anxiety generated as the conversation unfolds.

Those competing values are organizational. Leaders must constantly be aware of these competing values, the role that they play in unfolding organizational life, and the unique ways in which these issues must be handled in order that the organization does not get bogged down and sidetracked.

The Battle

Dusk was fast approaching on this second day of battle. Longstreet's corps had fought itself to a frazzle on Little Round Top, Devil's Den, the Wheatfield, and the Peach Orchard. But at 6 p.m., the division of Richard Anderson that A. P. Hill had leant Longstreet swung into action. First Cadmus Wilcox's Alabamians charged screaming out of the woods from Seminary Ridge and headed straight for the depleted lines of Winfield Hancock on Cemetery Ridge. Hancock had to buy at least a few minutes to bring up reinforcements to stem this flood of gray soldiers streaming toward his lines. The only troops available were the 1st

Minnesota regiment, which was flung into the fray, basically disintegrating in the maelstrom, but gaining Hancock just enough time to halt this attack.

Next came Ambrose Wright and David Lang's brigades as the en echelon attack of Longstreet continued to unfold and sweep toward the Union lines on Cemetery Ridge. Wright crested Cemetery Ridge and was poised to break the Union line in two. Longstreet's attack came much closer to success than most people realize. But largely due to Hancock's incredibly timely actions and the inability of the Confederates to coordinate assaults, the attack was repulsed.

Take Action on the Leadership Triangle

- Note this inventory of qualities of each of the three leadership areas. Note which of these you tend to easily utilize. Which domain contains the preponderance of your qualities? Tactical? Strategic? Transformational?

Tactical		Strategic		Transformational
Expert		Innovator		Facilitator
Concrete		Visionary		Relational
Fixer		Thinker		Collaborator
Get my hands dirty		Imagine		Negotiate with people
Confident		Vision caster		Creative
What's the problem?		What's the result?		What's the question?
I like to solve problems		I like to make plans		I like to view things from different angles
I prefer being trained		I prefer being inspired		I prefer free flowing conversation
I get things done		I anticipate needs		I am aware of conflict
I prefer check lists		I prefer general direction		I prefer gathering input

I like making decisions		I like delegation		I like consensus
I obey authority		I like having authority		I question authority
I am uncomfortable with ambiguity		I bring clarity out of chaos		I don't mind ambiguity
I follow directions well		I am an effective communicator		I am a good listener
I don't like anxiety		I like to be provocative		I don't mind moderate levels of anxiety
I like to learn		I like to grow		I like to adapt
My skills make others more effective		My skills make others better prepared for the future		My skills help others cope with change
I prefer doing my job with excellence		I prefer synthesizing ideas		I prefer leading people

- Which of these three leadership areas does your job require the most?
- Given your own profile as to where the preponderance of your preferred behaviors lies, where do you understand you will have the most difficulty leading (e.g., I will have difficulty with the strategic, seeing the future and where my organization needs to go)?

Chapter 6

Constructive Conflict

Did you realize that the highest functioning organizations, and the lowest functioning organizations, are both riddled with conflict? That's because conflict is a necessary and constructive thing, if it is handled properly. If it is not understood, it can tear an organization apart. It's much like fire in that respect. Fire can cook your food and heat your house. It can also burn your house down if it's not properly understood and brokered.

The Battle

War obviously involves conflict. What we sometimes fail to appreciate is the conflict that often develops internally within opposing armies. These internal conflicts can frequently have adverse consequences on the direction of the conflict and the ultimate outcome of the war. Take a moment with me to review what had unfolded the first two days of the battle, with a view toward the developing internal conflict in the southern army.

The Army of Northern Virginia had been dragged into a conflict on ground and with timing not of their choosing on the first day of July. But as night falls, the two bloodied armies faced each other across the farms, orchards, and woodlots to the south of the town of Gettysburg. The question for both generals was what to do now. General Meade has a somewhat easier decision. His troops were digging in on arguably one of the most defensible positions the Army of the Potomac had ever taken. Meade had desired a defensive position back in Maryland, north of Frederick at Pipes Creek. But that idea faded as the two armies tangled on the fields north and west of the village that first hot day in July. Now basically the consensus among his generals was to hold this new position and fight it out here.

On the other side of the line, there was much less consensus. Lee, in viewing the Union army digging in on the heights south of town, wanted to strike his foe there. His senior subordinate, General Longstreet, sharply disagreed. Longstreet figured (and would continue to figure for the next two days and, for that matter, the rest of his life) that the Federal position was basically impregnable, and the southern army needed to maneuver around the enemy, get in his rear, and establish a defensive position against which Meade could throw his army.

The conflict between the two generals would reach the boiling point on the morning of July 3 when Lee wanted Longstreet to lead the attack against the Union center. Longstreet thought the plan outlandish and protested bitterly. Lee merely pointed at the center of the Union position and told Longstreet that that was where the attack would fall, and Longstreet would lead it. Since then, some historians have speculated that part of the failure of the attack rested on the fact that Longstreet led it half-heartedly, without being in agreement with the plan (however it's hard to see how he was half-hearted when considering the ferocity of the attack he launched, which was basically as successful as the celebrated attack Stonewall Jackson had launched two months before at Chancellorsville).

Obviously, war is destructive. But healthy conflict where disagreement is entertained is critical to successful team functioning. The central conflict at Gettysburg was between Lee and Longstreet. Close behind this was the Meade-Sickles conflict. Both of these conflicts threatened the integrity of the two armies as the battle unfolded.

Remember Dan Sickles from chapter 4? He's the scoundrel political general in charge of the III Corps. Meade had put him way down below Cemetery Hill (where Meade mistakenly thought the southern attack would never fall on July 2) in what Meade considered the least important spot on the defensive line. Sickles took one look at his placement—

Cemetery Ridge—and descended from its namesake hill. As Cemetery Ridge approached the two Round Tops, it was no longer a ridge and, indeed, was more of a swale, lower than the ground to the west where arguably a southern assault could be launched. This terrain was where Sickles was placed.

Sickles was unhappy with this placement and completely disagreed with Meade. He argued his point but lost. But he found in Meade's words enough discretion that Sickles thought to move his corps out of alignment with the II Corps forming on his right up Cemetery Ridge to the cemetery at the top. When Union scouts reported possible enemy movements west of Sickles' position, he decided to march his men three fourths of a mile up into a peach orchard and spread them out, now satisfied that he had achieved a far superior position to defend. Unfortunately, this misalignment almost cost the Union its victory at the battle, for this is the very spot that Lee has sent Longstreet surreptitiously to strike and turn the Federal army.

When Meade learned of Sickles' insubordinate move, he rushed to correct it. But by the time he reached Sickles to order him back into alignment, Longstreet had launched his attack, and Sickles would have to stand and defend the ground he had chosen. For his efforts, Sickles' corps was practically destroyed; and only by the heroic efforts of many commanders, principally Winfield S. Hancock, were order and alignment restored to the Union line and the day salvaged.

Both the Army of Northern Virginia (Confederate) and the Army of the Potomac (Union) had histories of internal conflict that had distracted from the mission of both armies. A. P. Hill, a notoriously touchy general, had gotten into scraps with Generals Jackson and Longstreet, leading at one point to him being placed under arrest. Union generals had continually attempted to undercut the various commanding generals of the Army of the Potomac, at points going around him to complain directly to Lincoln.

General Lee was unusually conflict and confrontation averse (an obvious irony in that he was one of the most aggressive and audacious fighters in the history of warfare). The anxiety he evidently experienced in personal conflict with colleagues led him to take measures to avoid it *whenever possible. As a result, issues that should have been discussed and argued through were not thoroughly vetted.*

In the various organizations in which we consult, we find again and again the inability of leaders to confront and deal with conflict. Usually the course chosen is to devise a work around that bypasses the disagreement. Unfortunately, these jerry-rigged quick fixes themselves become problems.

We once worked with a leader who had difficulty with one of his direct reports coming in late virtually every day. The leader, rather than confront the problem and exercise his authority, decided to institute a time clock for everyone. Unfortunately, the rest of the organization felt they were not trusted and morale plummeted.

The Nature of Conflict

The highest performing, most effective teams are also the most highly conflicted teams, as are the poorest performing, least effective teams. How could this be? The issue is not the presence or absence of conflict. The issue has to do with how each of us handles conflict.

Embracing conflict as it arises in our life and in the life of those with whom we are most closely connected is the foundation for improving the quality of our relationships. How could this be? Remember what we've said about the well-defined leader—she/he has self-awareness. So let's look at the first principle of conflict:

- *Maybe the best place to learn about yourself is in the arena of conflict.*

   That's because conflict has the ability to elicit our most central personal issues that lie deep within our unique stories and the principles and values that we hold dear. These personal issues involve our core values as to what is most important to us and how we prioritize our lives. These issues also involve our aspirations and longings, our strivings, and our sense of inadequacy and failure. Unfortunately, for most people, these issues lie buried and unexamined, as we fight and argue with people around them in ways that are less than constructive.

And when it comes to leadership, conflict is neither a personal failure nor a distraction from your calling.

- *Conflict is your calling as a leader!*

  Conflict cannot be avoided. It's inherent in life itself, and especially the life of any organization. The apparent absence of conflict usually means that the conflict has gone underground because an overbearing leader demands compliance, and everyone remaining in the organization inadvertently agrees to be subservient. But leaders must have strong people, with definite opinions, who can challenge and defend and spar with the boss and one another over the various issues that confront any organization. When done properly, this brings clarity and enrichment to the discussion.[21]

If we used just a small portion of the time we waste in avoiding conflict, to learn the skills we need to resolve conflict in our self and with others, the world would be a different place! Leaders of the future need to have the stomach for conflict and uncertainty —among their people and within themselves. Unfortunately, for leaders of many organizations, especially those in existence for a long time, the situation usually points to a conflict allergy.

---

[21] Remember, there's a big difference between compliance (where people are compelled to go along with an idea) and commitment (where people have "bought in" to an initiative).

Transformational leaders of the future need to have the stomach for conflict and uncertainty, among their people and within themselves, precisely because our world has become ever faster paced, and uncertain, even as it continues to become more interconnected. That's why leaders of the future need to have an experimental mindset. Some decisions will work; some won't. Some projects will pay off; some won't. But every decision and every project will teach you and your organization something about how the world is changing. Every decision will have transformational elements that need to be wrestled with by stakeholders, and that will invariably involve conflict.

So let's take a look at conflict, and see how it can actually work for you, instead of being a demon lurking in the shadows, waiting to jump out and devour you.

Conflict: Good or Bad?
The Red Zone and the Blue Zone

Let's make some distinctions that will help us understand conflict and the way it can be helpful or destructive.[22]

Red zone	Blue zone
• This conflict is personal • It's about me! • Emotions rule without being acknowledged • I must protect myself because I'm feeling weak • Emotions are denied in self, therefore "projected" on others • The situation escalates	• This conflict is professional • It's about the business • The mission of the organization rules • I must protect the team and the business • Emotions are understood and acknowledged in myself • The situation is reframed into a more useful construct

---

[22] Look at a more in-depth discussion in *Red Zone, Blue Zone* by Osterhaus, Jurkowski, and Hahn.

Behaviors:	Behaviors:
✓ I disengage	✓ Thoughtful
✓ I become easily annoyed	✓ Reflective
✓ I'm resentful	✓ Listen deeply for what the underlying issue might be
✓ I procrastinate	✓ Do not see negative intent in other person
✓ I attack the other personally	
✓ I use alcohol as medication	
✓ I avoid people, situations	

Let's make a few comments about conflict. First, conflict per se is not good or bad. In fact the best *and* worst organizations are loaded with conflict. It's not the conflict; it's the *nature* of the conflict that is critical.

Conflict allows various points of view to emerge. It is absolutely essential for moving an organization forward. But remember, conflict is like fire—heating your house and cooking your food or burning the house down and destroying everything that is dear to you.

The Red Zone

Notice on the chart the characteristics of red zone conflict. This is conflict that is personal. In other words, the conflict is no longer about whatever issue we were disagreeing about. The issue is now *me*.

So the red zone is about my own personal issues and also about behavior. These behaviors, often learned in childhood, were originally designed to reduce the anxiety of a threatening situation. In adulthood, these coping strategy behaviors can be extremely effective in avoiding situations that create anxiety for us. While effective at reducing anxiety, they prevent us from making progress in our most important relationships.

Core Red Zone Issues

The personal nature of conflict (red zone) tends to assume a particular form for each of us depending on our personal wiring and the stories that shaped us (remember chapter 1). Take a look at the red zone forms or issues that people tend to have. Notice that there are only four.

Core issue	Self-description	Positive side	Negative side
Survival	"I must take care of myself. The world is full of peril, so I must enjoy the moment"	These people have traits of competence, self-reliance, and responsibility	These people lack the ability to trust others and tend to be wary and troubled in relationships. They have little interest in anything but what is of practical benefit. They become angry and panicky (red zone) whenever they feel their survival has been threatened
Acceptance	"I will do anything to be loved and accepted by others. I am a people pleaser"	These people have a heart for serving others and are very attentive to the needs and feelings of other people	These people are overly compliant and self-effacing. They tend to be rescuers. They become angry and carry personal grudges (red zone) whenever they feel they have been rejected
Control	"The world is a threatening place, and the only way I can feel safe is if I can control every situation and the people around me"	These people tend to have strong leadership qualities. They are vigilant, are highly organized, and have high expectations of themselves	These people often wall themselves off emotionally. They do not let others get too close to them. They can be overly controlling toward others—bossy, directive, demanding, rigid, and nit-picking. They impose perfectionist demands on others. They become anxious and angry (red zone) whenever anyone or anything threatens their control
Competence	"I am loved only on the basis of my performance. My performance is never good enough, so I never feel worthy of being loved"	These people tend to be high achievers. If you are a leader, you want these people on your team, because they will work hard to achieve a great performance	They are never satisfied with their achievements. They have a hard time receiving from other people. They impose perfectionist demands on themselves. They are defensive and easily angered (red zone) whenever they perceive that their competence has been questioned

Basically everyone can have all of these, but one is always going to be the favorite or signature or default red zone issue. A person can be a competence guy, but at the same time want to be accepted, and can be controlling at times. But competence would be considered the signature issue that drives that person as conflict arises. And the danger for this person, in a disagreement with someone, is that she will begin to read competence into the conflict—"Oh, you think I'm not competent!"

As conflict about a particular matter unfolds, people think they're still arguing about whatever the original issue was. But there's a subtle internal shift, as that person's personal issue from long ago in their personal story begins to activate.

There are two good ways to see when the conflict is red zone: First, the intensity in the conflict is disproportionate to the issue at hand, someone's shouting and screaming about an issue that seems inconsequential. Second, the conflict goes on far too long without resolution. The reason it can't get resolved is the original issue is no longer what the conflict is about. Red zone conflict, because it is about my personal issue, can *never* be resolved, certainly not by wrapping a totally unrelated issue in it that is submerged and personal to that particular combatant.

Red zone issues go back to childhood issues and subsequent values, attitudes, and behaviors. Those you need to resolve on your own. What's important for you to realize is how these issues get pulled into everyday conflicts and totally muck up the process of resolution. You see this everywhere—in political discourse, between husbands and wives, in board rooms, in shops, and in classrooms. Two people on the surface appear to be disagreeing about some hot political topic, or a future potential project, or a course of action. But it becomes more obvious that one or both of them has moved away from the propositional elements of the argument and slipped into more personal realms where emotion rules and reason disappears.

Red Zone Postures

Now let's take this a step further and look at red zone postures. I call these postures because so many people get confused and think only the blamers are in the red zone. So now look at this graph.

Posture	Hoped for results
Placating. Often done by acceptance people	So others won't be mad
Blaming. Often done by controlling people	So others will see me as strong
Computing. Often used by survival people	So others will see I'm not threatened
Distracting. Often used by competence people	So others will ignore the threat

This was adapted from Virginia Satir who was a family therapist a number of years ago. Notice that several of these postures don't really look like red zone, especially the computing posture. These people appear so very logical and rational. Yet, underneath, their own personal issues have been triggered. They've just learned to talk like Mr. Spock in the old *Star Trek*.

Let's use an example. Suppose you and I are arguing about the direction of a project. Good so far. But then somehow my red zone, which is acceptance, gets tweaked. So now I'm really trying to be accepted by you, not arguing the merits of my ideas about the project. And I start placating you, all the while you're blaming me for all manner of infractions, or disloyalty, or doing the project wrong, whatever.

If you're a blamer, you go on the attack. If you're a placater, you begin apologizing for your own indiscretions. If you're a computer, you start spouting facts and figures like a computer readout. And if you're a distractor, you tell a meaningless joke. But again, the true issue at hand being discussed is slowly lost, as personal issues for each combatant emerge and distract participants from authentically wrestling with the merits of that true issue.

The Blue Zone

The blue zone is established when people are able to do the following.

Self-awareness, including: Emotional self-awareness Accurate self-assessment Self-confidence Staying blue zone, not red zone	*Self-management in blue zone*: Emotional self-control Transparency Adaptability Achievement
Social awareness Empathy for other's point of view Organizational awareness	*Relationship management* Transformational leadership Influence Developing others Change catalyst Building bonds Teamwork and collaboration

Notice that the blue zone begins with my own self-awareness. As I become aware of myself, I can manage myself. After that, I can become more socially aware and am able to manage relationships—especially conflicted relationships. In this way, I am able to become the transformational leader. I can't lead transformationally unless I'm first in the blue zone. So the blue zone is the willingness to accept responsibility for all our behavior and the consequences of our behavior.

Blue zone is the continual refusal to shift responsibility for our actions to anyone or to any institution or to any system. Accepting responsibility for our behavior allows us to *change* the behavior that is inconsistent with our most personal values. And the inverse is also true! Accepting responsibility for our own behavior protects us from accepting responsibility for other's behavior.

Boundaries

Now let's consider boundaries. We touched on this in chapter 3. Let's unpack this more fully. Healthy boundaries identify and separate the self from others and consequently are the foundation of the blue zone. Boundaries are the fences, both physical and emotional, that mark off our world, creating zones of safety, authority, privacy, and territoriality. Boundaries are essential components because they:

- Define who we are—what we believe, think, feel, and do— where my story ends and yours begins
- Restrict access and intrusions
- Protect priorities
- Differentiate between personal (red zone) and professional (blue zone) issues.

Boundary difficulties go hand in hand with red zone issues. As I sink deeper into the morass of the red zone, my personal boundaries invariably are involved, and I engage others in my emotional drama in unhealthy ways.

For some people, boundaries become too rigid. Vital information—the lifeblood of any healthy person—is greatly restricted. Stylized ways of behaving become fixed. Prejudices are constructed and maintained.

For other people, boundaries become too porous or ambiguous. In such cases, the integrity and cohesion of the person are threatened by a lack of definition—"Who am I, other than an extension of you?"

We are used to the visible boundary markers of our world: fences, hedges, and traffic signs. Less obvious, but equally effective, are the internal boundaries that mark off emotional territory: "These are my thoughts, my feelings, my story" or "This is my responsibility, not yours." These internal boundaries are emotional barriers that protect and enhance the integrity of individuals.

A person can be so close-minded that no new thoughts and information reaches him. He can also be so loose with boundaries that he's swayed by every idea that comes along, never able to establish his own position on anything.

Boundaries are critical in understanding the red zone, because among other things, sinking into the red zone represents a boundary violation. When I am in conflict with another person, it is critical that my thoughts and emotions stay present to the issues upon which we disagree. When I permit old storylines to creep into the equation and color my feelings, I have violated a boundary. When I begin to see the other person as a person other than who she truly is (to be discussed below), I violate a boundary. For those people who have poor boundaries (too rigid or too porous), the dangers of red zoning are all the more prominent.

Here's a quick test to help you determine the strength and health of your own personal boundaries (based on ideas suggested by C. L. Whitfield in *Boundaries and Relationships*). See if you agree or disagree with the following statements:

Too porous

- ➢ I have difficulty making up my mind
- ➢ I have difficulty saying no to people
- ➢ I feel my happiness depends on other people
- ➢ I would rather attend to others than to myself
- ➢ Others' opinions are more important than mine
- ➢ People take and use my things without asking me
- ➢ I have difficulty asking for what I want or need
- ➢ I would rather go along with other people than express what I would really like to do
- ➢ It's hard for me to know what I think and believe
- ➢ I have a hard time determining what I really feel

> ➤ I don't get to spend much time alone
> ➤ I have a hard time keeping a confidence
> ➤ I am very sensitive to criticism
> ➤ I tend to stay in relationships that are harmful to me
> ➤ I tend to take on or feel what others are feeling
> ➤ I feel responsible for other people's feelings

Now let's see if your boundaries might be too rigid.

Too rigid

> ➤ My mind is always made up
> ➤ It is much easier for me to say no than to say yes to people
> ➤ My happiness never depends on other people
> ➤ I would rather attend to myself than to others
> ➤ My opinion is more important than others'
> ➤ I rarely if ever lend my things to other people
> ➤ Most issues appear very black and white to me
> ➤ I know exactly what I think and believe on almost every issue
> ➤ I have a hard time determining what I really feel
> ➤ I spend much time alone
> ➤ I keep most of my thoughts to myself
> ➤ I am immune to criticism
> ➤ I find it difficult to make and maintain close relationships
> ➤ I never feel responsible for other people's feelings

Creating Healthy Boundaries

Creating healthy boundaries is absolutely critical to optimal functioning as a leader. Let's consider several steps to achieving healthy boundaries, first those that are internal to you, then those that are external.

Steps to creating healthy internal boundaries:

To be successful as leaders, we must be well defined. Being well defined assumes healthy personal boundaries. So let's look at several elements that will help us move toward more healthy personal boundaries. These include first the internal boundaries, then the external boundaries.

- Learn to recognize your own emotional responses.
- Become aware of when you are reacting to an authority figure, a peer, or a situation in an inappropriate manner.
- Become aware when the other is reacting to something in you.
- Recognize situations in which you repeat the same behavior and produce the same result.
- Recognize situations that create anxiety for you and acknowledge that fear to self.
- When a conflict arises, talk about your behavior and feelings with someone. Avoid focusing on the other person's behavior.
- Become aware of the people who provoke emotional responses in you.
- Identify the characteristics in that person that provoke the emotional response in you: e.g., he is so arrogant or so needy or so angry.
- Recognize that if you are unable to resolve an issue with someone after talking about it, then there is another deeper level conflict present.
- If you realize that another issue is present, acknowledge that and get support from a third party.

Steps to creating healthy external boundaries:
- Understand your target audience and anticipate what the resistance will be.
- When you experience resistance from others, avoid personalizing the situation.

- Ask questions in a nonthreatening manner and genuinely seek to understand the issues.
- Do not respond in the moment if you are feeling threatened.
- Determine when you need help, what kind, how much, and from whom.
- Create a safe environment.
- Be aware of team values when attacked from outside.
- Don't assume same things work for all.
- Use dry runs for briefings.
- Give and get feedback.
- Ask for help.
- Constantly share information.
- Create more clarity around task and purpose.
- Create more clarity around roles and responsibility.
- Have an understanding and tolerance for various work styles.
- Be better at giving and receiving feedback.
- Show support for each other.
- Include more peer review.

A Word About Blue Zone Staff Meetings

Now let's take a moment to consider staff meetings and how these can be conducted in the blue zone. I want you to consider as you conduct your staff meetings that meetings are often time-consuming and unprofitable. Agendas wander. Red zone conflict emerges. People find excuses to absent themselves whenever possible. Let's look at an alternative, staff meetings in the blue zone. Look at the following questions below to get a sense of how your meetings have been unfolding.

Staff meetings in the blue zone

➢ Do our staff meetings actually have a purpose?
➢ Do we have more than one purpose?
➢ Do we have a clear agenda?

> ➤ Do we stay on the agenda?
> ➤ Do we allow the agendas of individual staff members to drive our meetings?
> ➤ Is the humor in our meetings helpful or distracting and defusing?
> ➤ Do we have clear goals?
> ➤ Are the goals measurable?
> ➤ Do we measure the goals?
> ➤ Do we hold each other accountable for meeting our goals?

A Word About Avoidance of Conflict

As we have stated, some people are allergic to conflict. As a result, they avoid it at all costs, even when healthy disagreement and conflict will bring about a more robust solution to a problem. *Lee, as we have stated, was evidently allergic to personal conflict (though he pitched right in to war in a very audacious manner). When he saw Longstreet balk at his plan on the second day to march south and hit the Union army in the flank, Lee turned to Longstreet's subordinate (stepping out of the hierarchy), Lafayette McLaws. In Longstreet's presence, Lee assumed Longstreet's role and advised McLaws as to how to proceed in executing the plan.*

In my role as an executive coach, I have been called in by some leaders to "coach" a supposed recalcitrant subordinate. More often than not, the leader who contacted me has refused to confront the subordinate about alleged poor performance. In such cases, I find that the leader is actually the one needing coaching. In these cases, I help the leader understand his own aversion to conflict, while pointing out the essential nature of it in ongoing organizational life.

Karpman Drama Triangle

Internalized conflict can lead to the drama triangle. Drama triangles appear in all organizations, but especially in those organizations that are less healthy and driven by chronic anxiety within the organizational system. Note the triangle below.

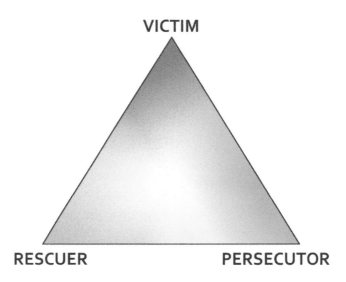

VICTIM

RESCUER   **PERSECUTOR**

The model posits three habitual psychological roles which people often take in a situation:

- The person who is treated as, or accepts the role of, a *victim*.
- The person who pressures, coerces, or *persecutes* the victim.
- The *rescuer* who intervenes out of an ostensible wish to help the situation or the underdog.
- The victim is not really as helpless as he feels, the rescuer is not really helping, and the persecutor does not really have a valid complaint.

The drama plays out with the protagonist starting off in one of the three main roles: rescuer, persecutor, or victim, with the other principal player (the antagonist) in one of the other roles. Thereafter, "the two players move around the triangle, thus switching roles," so that, for example, the victim turns on the rescuer or the rescuer switches to persecuting.

The covert purpose for each "player" is to get their unspoken (and frequently unconscious) psychological wishes/needs met in a manner they feel justified, without having to acknowledge the broader dysfunction or harm done in the system as a whole. As such, each player is acting upon his own selfish "needs," rather than acting in a genuinely responsible or altruistic manner.

The Battle

The setting sun has mercifully put an end to the horrific scene that had been the second day of fighting at Gettysburg. The small farms of Gettysburg's citizenry lay in ruins. Fields trampled. Woodlots blasted to splinters. The battlefield was a mass of dead and writhing humanity among the discarded accouterments of war. Surgeons quickly established operating theaters wherever they could find a suitable spot, with regimental bands stationed outside and ordered to play as loudly as possible to mask the screams of the wounded from the rest of the troops.

The two opposing generals now faced the same daunting decision: What to do on the morrow? Should I attack? Should I hold my position and wait to be attacked? Should I withdraw from this place and seek a more advantageous situation and continue the fight there? The two generals would go about making this momentous decision in two very different ways. Lee had had strong disagreement with Longstreet as to the best course of action. His other two corps commanders were too inexperienced for him to seek their advice. Lee would take counsel within himself and inform subordinates of his decision, thus avoiding the conflict. This decision, made in the absence of any dissenting opinions and comments, would prove disastrous to the southern cause.

Meade would hold a late night council of war with his principal subordinates and actually take a vote as to what was the best course of action. There was evidently a great deal of uncertainty on the part of Meade as to exactly what he should do (partly due to his newness to com-

mand of the army). And the 145,000 men still left in both armies would settle down that night to a very uneasy sleep, not knowing what to expect when the dawn beckoned to them.

Take Action in Your Understanding of Conflict

- Consider ongoing conflicts continually have emerged in your family. List each conflict, how it was handled, and how each conflict could have been handled more effectively.

Conflicted incident	How conflict was handled	How conflict could have been handled more effectively

- Consider ongoing conflicts that continually have emerged in your leadership. List each conflict, how it was handled, and how each conflict could have been handled more effectively.

Conflicted incident	How conflict was handled	How conflict could have been handled more effectively

- What has been the general style, an acceptable leadership team style, of dealing with conflict in the past (e.g., as a team, we usually avoid conflict at all costs, or we usually end up in the senior leader's office and she decides who is to blame)?

- Are difficult issues raised on the leadership team without becoming adversarial? Or if adversarial, does the conflict tend to remain blue zone?
- What usually happens to you personally when difficult issues arise?
- What is your influence on the team and vice versa as these difficult situations are unfolding (e.g., the team seeks to dive into the situation, which raises my anxiety even higher, and I end up distracting the team)?
- Write down your core red zone issue as you understand it and how it affects you personally. Note that everyone can experience all four themes. But one theme usually stands out as the dominant or signature theme, the other three subordinating to that theme.

Internalizing Conflict

Look at some of the symptoms that occur when you internalize conflict. That is, you take it on board and dwell on it instead of externalizing it where it can be worked through and resolved. Put a check by those you have used.

- o   Work harder
- o   Be quiet/withdraw
- o   Send e-mail rather than talk
- o   Reluctantly comply
- o   Rebel against each other
- o   Become uncooperative
- o   Find solace outside organization
- o   Overanalyze
- o   Second guess your actions/intentions
- o   Get depressed
- o   Blame! (yourself, others, and the system)
- o   Try to exert more control
- o   Protect your own turf

o   Build in more structure/rules
o   Respond immediately to outside demands
o   Short circuit established communication chains
o   Deny, escape, make excuses, overeat
o   Develop illnesses (mental and physical to avoid the issues)
o   Distrust everything and everyone

Part III

The Third Day

The battle had raged for two days. The countryside around Gettysburg had been devastated—fields trampled, woodlots blasted, and homes pockmarked from bullets and shell fragments. The stench of rotting flesh was omnipresent. The normal background sounds of birds could not be heard, as most had fled to safer climes. A tension hung over the surrounding environs, the sense that the maelstrom had not yet run its course. The two armies still faced one another—tense, determined, and lethal.

Lee's aggressiveness had not faltered. He saw the enemy on the ridge in front of him, and his determination to get at them mounted. Lee had taken counsel only within himself. He had not consulted his principal commanders, two of whom were brand new to corps command and one (Longstreet) who has been in near complete disagreement with his plans since the onset of the battle. But Lee had been successful in the past when he had seized the initiative, and his confidence in his troops remained strong. Longstreet's flank attack the previous day had nearly broken the Federal lines. He would use the same strategy that had been successful in the past, with the men he considered to be invincible.

Meade anticipated his enemy's next move. He was well dug in on the high ground, and after a late night meeting with his principal generals where he solicited their advice, he had determined to stay put and allow Lee to make the next move. He had surmised that Lee would attempt to hit him in the center, where Hancock's II Corps was firmly anchored.

The morning of Friday, July 3, saw the temperature rise through the eighties. The sky was clear. Lee summoned his principal commanders together to apprise them of his plan of attack. And yes, he had consistently determined to attack, to not alter his initial plan since arriving on this field two days ago. His mind had fixated on what he deemed to be the successful approach to this battle. He would not change his plan.

We have seen how the well-defined leader is one who is able to build trust, one who understands the organization as a whole, and thus is more effectively able to align the organization as he recognizes the three facets of leadership and respond accordingly and deal effectively with conflict. It is these leaders who are most successful responding for the need for change.

Chapter 7

How to Bring About Change in a Diverse Environment

Yes, we live in a world where change comes rapidly. There was a book written a generation ago, *Future Shock,* which explained how the acceleration of change in modern times leaves people, as they attempt to adjust, in a state of shock. But change is inevitable, and our ability to respond appropriately is critical.

The American Civil War has been called the last of the ancient wars and the first of the modern wars. It was a war that introduced the first metallic rifle and pistol cartridges, the first repeating rifles and carbines, the first war where troops were moved by railroad, the first ironclad ships, and many other inventions which heralded a change in warfare. But the military still relied on the old tried and trusted means of smoothbore muskets, paper cartridges, and troops marching in military precision across the battlefield toward the enemy. More innovations and experimentation took place during the Civil War than during all other previous wars combined. Generals and senior grade officers alike were constantly required to make changes in their basic ways of thinking about how war should be conducted.

The Battle

As Lee rode into the outskirts of Gettysburg on the late morning of July 1, the first day of the great battle that had already begun to unfold, he could reflect back on his last thirteen months that had been characterized by one transition after another. Some of the changes he had experienced had been brought about by circumstances—he had been a military advisor until a shell fragment had removed Joe Johnston from command of the southern army in the east, and he had been thrust into that position. Then there were the changes that he himself had brought about by his own initiative, first taking the army he had inherited and thrusting it against the Union army which had penetrated to the suburbs of Richmond. He had taken careful note of which commanders performed to his standards and elevated them. He had removed others and generally restructured his army around two corps: Longstreet commanding the first, Stonewall Jackson the second.

Then in May of 1863, at the battle of Chancellorsville, a bullet had felled Jackson, and pneumonia had taken his life, and Lee was left with only one corps commander he trusted: Longstreet. He had decided to divide Jackson's II Corps into two, giving one to A. P. Hill, the other to Dick Ewell. He rode into southern Pennsylvania with this organization in place.

The first two days of July had now passed, and Lee had witnessed some of the fiercest and bloodiest fighting the war had produced. As the dawn broke over the Adams County countryside just south of Gettysburg's town limits on the third day of battle, Lee stood staring at the Union lines. Longstreet, Lee's steady trusted lieutenant, gazed at the same lines nearly a mile away. Longstreet's conclusion was those Federal lines were impregnable. Best to leave them alone, swing around behind them, and get into a strong defensive position. Longstreet surmised there was still time to do that. But Longstreet also undoubtedly worried that Lee's "fighting blood" was now up, and Lee would never relinquish this field if another aggressive attack would carry the day and win the battle. This had been precisely the winning formula four weeks earlier at Chancellorsville—strike them in their flank, then hit them up the middle. Weren't the two situ-

ations essentially the same? Longstreet thought not. But Lee would hear none of it. And besides, Longstreet had not been at Chancellorsville, and he did not experience firsthand that victory (a potentially good reason to heed Longstreet's insights and not go with your own instincts).

Lee was going to send General Pickett from Longstreet's corps, and Pettigrew supported by Trimble from Hill's corps right into the middle of the Union line. Surely that part of their line was weakened with attacks having fallen on both flanks. And Lee had the finest fighting units the world had ever seen, right?

Longstreet had a daunting task the morning of July 3: change Lee's mind as to how to proceed with this battle. Ever since the two armies had engaged on the first of July, Lee had assumed an aggressive, offensive posture. Longstreet had tried unsuccessfully during the first two days of battle to discourage Lee from this posture, which Longstreet surmised to be ultimately disastrous. We'll never know exactly what was in Lee's mind that third of July morning. He left no record and spoke to no one as to whether he had seriously entertained a change in his overall attack mentality. We do know that Longstreet engaged him in a quite definitive manner (Longstreet never acted as the compliant subordinate in any appreciable way during the entirety of the war), attempting to get him to alter his thinking. But the more Longstreet pushed, the more adamant Lee's position became. "The enemy is there [pointing to the center of the Union line on Cemetery Ridge], and I intend to attack him." End of the matter.

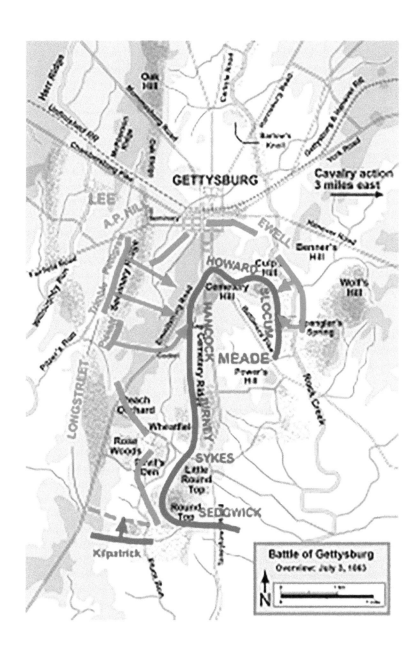

Keeping Our Bearings as Things Change

Well-defined leaders help people face the need for change and help them navigate stormy seas, all the while making needed changes in their own lives as changing circumstances demand different approaches. Two questions that the leader must constantly ask are as follows: What essential elements need to be retained? What's expendable? There are certain values and processes that are so central to the organization's core that to lose them would mean to lose the identity of the organization. What are these elements, and which assumptions, investments, processes, and policies need to be considered for radical change?

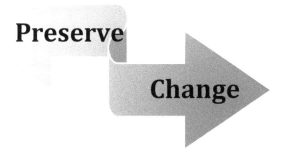

Abraham Lincoln (as we shall see in chapter 9) had to ask his countrymen: What's most precious about America? What values do we stand for? Do we stand for freedom and equal opportunity? Or do we stand for the principles by which we are living today? Obviously these questions were generating major conflict within the nation. In fact, the nation was in the process of tearing itself apart, attempting to answer these very questions. People faced an internal contradiction between the values they espoused and the way they lived. Millions of people had to decide for themselves what was precious about their country and what was expendable.

One can imagine the difficult conversations that have been held in corporate boardrooms from General Motors to Microsoft as these companies have had to face the brutal realities of these times. How do we restructure? How do we jettison time-honored product lines? How do we retool for the future? What processes, now in place, need to be reengineered lest they destroy us? These questions coupled with the concurrent question: what do we retain that is essential to our organization's code?

How to Bring About Change

Over time, the structures, culture, and defaults that make up an organizational system become deeply ingrained, self-reinforcing, and very difficult to reshape. Most organizations get trapped because these processes worked in the past. Our brains feel most secure when the tried and true road is selected. Anxiety rises as we select new roads to travel, requiring new maps, new tools, new processes to get us to our desired future. And as that anxiety reaches a certain threshold, all bets are off. We default to those tried and true, blinding ourselves and often those around us to a wider array of solutions and ideas that could create more value.

Successful individuals and organizations navigate transitions and respond effectively to changing conditions. They confront the brutal realities that life has a way of producing. Transitions are constantly occurring within all types of organizations—people come and people go. Relationships change. Boundaries, leadership, and communication styles are affected. People who relate to one another must negotiate new ways of dealing with each other. The culture is constantly shifting and evolving, demanding new responses in ever shorter time frames. The danger of changing times is that some individuals, and often the relational network as a whole, resist or ignore the changes and transitions that must be made. That resistance to change often creates a crisis within the organization—and danger often lurks within that crisis atmosphere, looking to destabilize and scuttle the organization as it navigates the rocky shoals and foaming white water of change.

The well-defined leader is one who is able to confront the brutal facts, beginning with the brutal facts of who he actually is—he is self-aware. What makes this so difficult for leaders is the fact that each of us has our own blind spots, our own competing values, our own subtle compromises that lie hidden because of our brain's inability to deal with the anxiety thus generated. Our brains go about constructing elaborate ruses that in the short term reduce the anxiety, but leave us poorly defined and incongruent.

A situation presents itself to our organizations (families, agencies, corporations, nonprofits). The situation demands that we initiate a change in our structure, our processes, our personnel, and our compensation schemes, often in our belief systems that undergird our values. The anticipated change conjures the losses we will sustain as a result of the change. Anxiety is generated. We back away from the change. We rationalize, "We've done just fine on the present course. I see no need to change now." If the role of the leader is first to help people face reality and then to mobilize them to make change, then the first step must be taken by the leader in considering herself, her own cherished beliefs, values, and ways of behaving.

The S Curve

Every organization has opportunities for new growth (S curve). Many organizations have used the S curve to plot the growth and development to maturity of their groups. The essence of the S curve, as applied to organizational development and transitions, is that organizations live through three major phases.

Phase I is the inception or formation phase, typically characterized by an innovative leader that drives the organization with a new idea. Creativity and experimentation abound during this phase because the people in the organization are trying to figure out how to be successful. Once the "formula" for success is discovered, the organization enters Phase II.

Phase II is the growth phase. As the organization grows and becomes more and more successful, the "formula" for success becomes ingrained into the organization's culture. Since everything around us tells us that what we're doing is correct, change becomes more and more difficult. People promoting change are labeled as problematic and are welcomed with the proverbial: "You cannot argue with success!" However, to the surprise of some (typically in management), sooner or later the organization's growth rate starts to decline; doing more of the same thing does not help. The organization approaches Phase III.

Phase III is the renewal phase. The organization is faced with two fundamental options: reinvention or death. The path to death takes many forms. For some, it's an obsessive pursuit of efficiency and cost cutting with little investment on generating new products or services. If it's 1920 and you're still manufacturing buggy whips while people are buying cars, I don't care how quality perfect or inexpensive your whips are, unless you reinvent your business, you're going to disappear. For others, death is the unavoidable consequence of denial, a negation of customer preferences, or blindness to an emerging need (Ulises Pabon, 2009). See the graphic representation below of the possible permutations of the S curve:

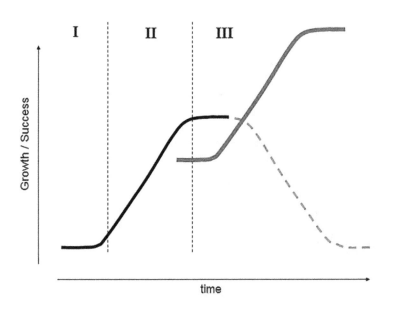

Reinvention allows the organization to realign around a compelling new vision and move it forward toward its desired future, all well and good. But we're going to suggest there are actually three problems:

1.   Our own propensity to sabotage change.
2.   Those around us in the organization's resistance to change.
3.   The leaders above us disrupting and sabotaging change.

Let's begin by looking at ourselves and the propensity that each of us has to sabotage *ourselves* as we avoid change.

Competing Values: How I Continually Manufacture *Non*-change

Let's start with how we in fact resist change—how we ourselves tend to resist the very changes we *ourselves* say we want to make. To do this, we need to turn back to our discussion of values. Remember, values are those things that matter most to us. Most of us would hope that our values are always aligned and consistent. Unfortunately, that is rarely the case.

Every organization—business, government agency, church, or club—holds numerous challenges as these go about conducting their missions. That will always be true. But what is it within myself that these myriad challenges elicit? It may be nearly impossible for us to bring about any important change in an organization without changing ourselves.

Two transformational challenges appear when it comes to values that each of us must face:

1.   The gap between the values we aspire to (and sometimes espouse, thinking we actually live by these) and the reality of how we actually behave (the stuff of incongruence that we talked about earlier)
2.   The competing commitments and the attached values that we constantly face

The Gap Between Aspired Values and Our Behavior

Ask anyone what is most important to them, what are the principles by which they lead their lives, and what are their core values if you will, and people will come up with a tidy list of five or six items that they say are their core principles. They'll mention things like treating everyone the same, or maintaining integrity, or being flexible, or exercising patience. Some people are able to admit that these are values to which they aspire. Others will swear that they live by these values and never deviate.

Let's walk through several statements and see how competing values may in fact be blocking you from going forward in those things that are most important to you.

1 I am committed to the value or importance of	2 What I'm doing or not doing that prevents my commitment in no 1 from being fully realized	3 Underneath, I have this competing commitment (value) that drives no. 2	4 Big assumption. The consequence generated if I actually perform no. 1.
More open and direct communication	I don't speak up when people violate the norm I value. I also talk behind people's back	Not being seen as a brave crusader, jerk, holier than thou	People did see me as a brave crusader or jerk, then I'd have no connections in my office and work would be a nightmare
Supporting my staff to be empowered and exercise more individual initiative	When I delegate an initiative to a subordinate, my anxiety rises as I see their subpar performance, and I micromanage the initiative	Empowering my staff means I lose quality control, and it's essential I be fully competent in all I produce	The quality of my work, when I transfer authority, will fall below what I would produce when I'm in control, and I'm a complete failure

152

I need to encourage conflict in order to entertain differing points of view	I avoid all conflict at any cost	Harmony is paramount to me and to how I see a smooth-running organization	If I get into conflict, then I will find myself becoming uncontrollably angry at catastrophic results
My stated values. What I aspire to. What I care about. A genuinely held commitment	My own part in this mess. How I sabotage myself! My own behavior that is directly contrary to what I state I'm committed to	My non-advertised competing value that drives the sabotage and in the process maintains the status quo and is largely unconscious	The catastrophe I anticipate will befall me, laden with a great deal of emotion

Look first at the top row: 1 through 4. Note the progress. I'm committed to one value (no. 1), but then (no. 2) I in fact do/don't do something that sabotages no. 1. That's because of no. 3, a competing value underneath no. 2, is fueled by a big assumption (no. 4).[23] To read the four columns backward tells a powerful story, holding to a big assumption (no. 4), we are understandably committed to protecting ourselves (no. 3) and maintaining the status quo. As we faithfully live out these commitments, we act in a particular fashion (no. 2). This in turn compromises our ability to truly realize our genuinely held commitments and values (1).

Another way to look at it is as follows: Column no. 1 are the values to which I aspire. Column no. 3 are the values I actually use when I'm deciding to act in any particular way. And unfortunately, column no. 3 trumps column no. 1, and I'm left with an incongruent message: *I really want to empower you, but darn it, if I do that, I'll end up compromising my other value of complete competence in all that I do. So I'll tell you I'll empower you, all the while micro-managing you.*

---

[23]   Adapted from Kegan and Lahey, *How the Way We Talk Can Change the Way We Work*

Notice that much of what we've talked about involves delegation. Delegation is extremely important for leaders. However, so many leaders get into micro-managing. There is undoubtedly a competing value at work inside of these managers, unless they simply believe that micro-managing is the absolute best way to manage their people, no matter how competent they might be.

Competing Commitments:
When One Value Trumps Another

It's important for you to begin to see how one value (e.g., empowerment/delegation) gets trumped by another value (competence). Think for a moment of what that competing value inside of the micro-managing managers is. There's a good chance that their need to be competent may be the competing value. It could also be the competing value of control. What happens when you delegate? You cede control. You know how you would perform, but what about those under you? Will they do an equally good job? The only way to know is to constantly look over their shoulder, thus maintaining control.

Realize that not all column no. 1 values are aspired values. Often there is a trumping of one value by an equally valid second value, and it just turns out that both values are brought into play at the same time around a certain issue. Look at the list below. These are valid values trumped by equally valid values. I truly hold the value of transparency and tend to live that out. But certain situations mitigate against transparency, such as when there is a person or an initiative that needs to be held in confidence. Or I truly value innovation, but often that is trumped within me by the need to be efficient (which demands consistency) or safety.

Remember the list of competing values we enumerated in chapter 5:

- Quality *versus* quantity
- Efficiency *versus* innovation
- Protection *versus* challenge

- Consistency *versus* variety
- Expansion *versus* preservation
- Transparency *versus* confidentiality
- Commonality *versus* difference
- Individual considerations *versus* community considerations

Note that one of the two values is aspired, and the other is the actual value used in decision-making. Both are utilized by the person at various times. But now a decision needs to be made: we need to protect our people within this organization and not let them go *versus* our bottom line keeps shrinking and salaries are our highest line item. Or, I want to be totally transparent with my people, but there are certain things that I just can't share, or I'll compromise various critical initiatives to our business. These competing values can only be managed; they can never be adequately solved. And we can remain congruent as long as we first admit to ourselves, and then to those we lead, that we are caught in this competing values conundrum and will need to intentionally navigate this going forward.

When Those Around Us Sabotage

So hopefully we understand that we're actually internally wired to resist change, and we will fight change, then will go about justifying our actions to continue to make ourselves appear in the best light. To tell you the truth, our own resistance within ourselves, concerning competing values, is in many ways more interesting than the resistance we get from others. But we need to get clear on others' resistance.

Here's a motto that's worth remembering: resistance is your ally. That's right; when people resist you and try to sabotage you, those behaviors should actually be seen as allies, an ally because it's giving you information, nothing more, nothing less. But it tends to screw up my plans for moving forward.

However, a better way to understand it is merely the forces that exist within each of us that resist change. Remember what we said, our brains are structured in such a way as to feel most comfortable during steady state, when nothing is altered. Introduce the hint of change, and anxiety rises as our brains tend to react and resist.

The first signal resistance sends is this: *I don't like this change.* In fact, I don't like *any* change. The second thing resistance signals is this: *Okay, I can tolerate some change, but you're going too fast!* When the signal inside of us activates, it is up to us to figure out what the signal means. The same as when your smoke detector goes off in your house late at night. You can say to yourself, "Damn smoke detector," while you rip it off the wall and destroy it. Or you can try to figure out what the detector is signaling to you. If there's a fire, you sure want to know about it.

Take a look at some of the guises that signal resistance.

Resistance comes in many semblances. We usually think of it as the in-your-face kind of words and actions. But that's only a part of it. People resist in all kinds of clever ways, mainly depending on their upbringing and personalities. Arguably, it's the passive resistance that is more effective—like silence or easy agreement—simply because it's so sinister. You never quite know what you're fighting.

Guises of resistance

- ✓ *Confusion*: "So why are we doing this (after many explanations)?"
- ✓ *Immediate criticism*: "What a dumb idea."
- ✓ *Denial*: "I don't see any problem here."
- ✓ *Malicious compliance*: "I concur completely and wholeheartedly."
- ✓ *Sabotage*: "Let's get him!"
- ✓ *Easy agreement*: "No problem."
- ✓ *Deflection*: "What do you think the Cubs' chances are this year?"
- ✓ *Silence*
- ✓ *In-your-face criticism*: "You're the worst pastor we've ever had!"

Handling resistance

✓ *Maintain clear focus*:
  • Keep both long and short view, one eye on the goal and one on the present moment.
  • Persevere. Hang in there.
✓ *Embrace resistance (remember, it's my ally!)*:
  • Move toward the resistance. Keep in mind resistance always signals that the resistant person is expressing internal conflict. The voice of resistance tells you what's wrong. The most resistant person is merely the voice for others. Once you know why people are concerned, you can attempt to find common ground. Knowing objections unlocks possibilities.
  • Hear the reasons beneath the reasons. People fear change.
✓ *Respect those who resist*:
  • Continually monitor your red zone.
  • Listen with interest. Resistors may have important things to teach us.
✓ *Join with the resistance*:
  • Look for ways that the "game" needs to change.

Now look at how we handle resistance:

Resistance tends to signal that there are transformational issues under the surface (because anxiety has been generated by the anticipated losses). That's one of the great benefits of resistance. It's the most effective signal for the presence of transformational issues. What we find over and over is that people apply technical solutions to transformational problems. And that never works. So when you apply a technical solution, and the resistance continues, or the solution becomes the problem, that should tell you that transformational issues are lurking somewhere in the bushes.

Let's say that you just got an e-mail from your supervisor telling you that for some reason you will have to move the office of eleven people you manage to a location across the street. Okay, no problem. Technical problem. So you go about moving preparations and call a staff meeting. In the meeting, you get all kinds of push back on moving office locations, and several people don't attend the meeting saying they "forgot." "It's just across the street!" You protest. No good. The resistance intensifies. Now you could go red zone at this point and assume all of this resistance is in response to your competence or is questioning your authority. Or you could stay blue zone and realize that there is an transformational issue here lurking. That it's not just about moving furniture. That's how resistance should act as a signal to you.[24]

Most people end up butting their heads against the resistance instead of listening to the signal, intuiting what it is saying, and deciding what next to do. Your job as a leader is to find themes and possibilities. You've got to be able to stay blue zone—to realize it's not about you, it's about the mission.

So, in relation to the moving across the street problem, the manager can do two things: she can see the resistance as about her and get defensive and start abusing the resistors for putting up such a stink about something so minor as a move, or she can say something like the following:

> Folks, I know that any move can be upsetting. And because we're moving across the street, I know that there are going to be losses for all of us. One thing lost is familiarity of surroundings. Another is the informal networks here in this building, people we know and trust and can actually rely on to get certain tasks done for us.

---

[24] One possible transformational issue in this scenario is the anticipated loss of informal relationships and network systems that exist at the present location. All of these will be altered or ended when the move occurs.

All of that competes with the needs of our organization to be more efficient with space so that we can continue to be profitable. You all are the ones who will experience the losses of this move, so let's talk about it, and see what can be done to make this go more smoothly for all of you.

Here's a quiz that should help point up some of those areas internally that might still be tripping you up as you face resistance.

- What things really set me off and cause me to overreact?
- Do I read other people's minds? Who? When do I read them? What is occurring?
- What do I fear the most? Rejection? Loss of control? Incompetence? Abandonment?
- What people or things do I hate the most?
- What characteristics do I find myself disliking in others (especially those of the same sex)? Is there one person in my life that I really can't stand? What is it about him/her, what characteristics, that set me off?
- What things do I know about myself that I try hard to keep hidden, even from those closest to me?
- What things do I *never* do, even though doing them may benefit me?
- What "strengths" do I have that, being preoccupied with them, may prevent me from being real and having fulfilling relationships (e.g., always care-taking others prevents me caring for myself.)?
- What are the themes of my dreams? Who is doing what?
- What do others say about me, especially those closest to me (spouse, friends, parents)? How am I perceived in the organization?
- Think back on a recent hardship, a loss of something truly important to you (spouse, friendship, job, status). What issues emerged? What was said to you?

The Battle

Lee hurled Pickett's division from Longstreet's corps, along with two divisions from A. P. Hill's corps, against the Union center. The attack was preceded by the largest artillery barrage that had ever been mounted on the continent. One hundred seventy southern cannon opened fire at once. The sound created could be heard over one hundred miles away. Shells screamed into and over the Union lines, creating havoc behind the front lines.

Then Confederate infantry emerged from the tree line along Seminary Ridge, a mile west of the Union lines. Twelve thousand men in gray and butternut stepped out and headed for the foe. As the Confederates approached, the men of Hancock's II Corps opened fire. In the Union center, the commander of artillery had held fire during the Confederate bombardment, leading southern commanders to believe the northern cannon batteries had been knocked out. However, they opened fire on the Confederate infantry during their approach with devastating results. Nearly one half of the attackers did not return to their own lines. Although the Federal line wavered and broke temporarily at a position called the "angle" in a low stone fence, reinforcements rushed into the breach, and the Confederate attack was repulsed. The farthest advance of Brig. Gen. Lewis A. Armistead's brigade of Maj. Gen. George Pickett's division at the angle is referred to as the "high-water mark of the Confederacy," symbolically representing the closest the South ever came to its goal of achieving independence from the Union via military victory.

Organizational history is replete with examples of failed initiatives, so many of which went awry because of the failure of leadership to change strategy, to change personnel, to change perspective on the situation. Change flies in the face of our brain's natural tendency to maintain the status quo, the familiar, the tried and true. And yet, as General Shinseki[25] once said, "If you don't like change, you're going to like irrelevance even less."

---

[25] General Eric Shinseki was the US army chief of staff from 1999 to 2003.

Take Action for Change

Answer the following questions:

- Do you understand how you set goals for yourself, then go about creating non-change because of internal competing values?
- Do you understand the role of resistance and how to handle it?
- Do you know the basics of how to lead change effectively?
- Are meetings designed primarily for decision-making or information sharing? Is there room for creative thought and learning from mistakes, or are they mostly for getting direction from the authority?
- If decisions are made at the meetings, what is the decision rule? How are decisions made? Do members discuss and then advise the chair, leaving the decision to her, or is a majority, supermajority, or consensus required for decisions? How does the decision-making rule reflect the context and purpose of the decision? Are all decisions made by one rule, or are different rules used for different problems and situations?
- Are attendees authorized to speak on subjects beyond their own areas of expertise? If so, are the new ideas integrated into thinking or just noise? Do people value nonjudgmental brainstorming, out-of-the-box ideas, and far-out possibilities?
- To what extent are attendees expected or required to share the meeting's content with their subordinates? When the information is shared, what work is done to integrate the information into the current reality?
- What role does the most senior person in the room play during the meeting? (Facilitator? Decision maker? Inquisitor? Provocateur?) Does the person create space for conflict or marginalize it?

Chapter 8

Managing Our People

Raising Up the Next Generation of Leadership

One of the most important roles of senior leadership is to manage what is arguably the most important asset the organization possesses: the people who work there. And one of the most critical aspects of the management of talent is identifying and engaging the up-and-coming leaders, then fostering their leadership and decision-making. That's how an organization grows. That's also how an organization is able to drive its most important values and ideas down into the organization. That's how it sustains its success.

The Battle

As Lee pulled out of Gettysburg on a rainy July 4, it is reported that his ambulance train reached to seventeen miles in length. His army was defeated. Nearly a third of Lee's generals were dead, soon to be dead, wounded, or captured. Confederate generals were killed included Semmes, Barksdale, Armistead, Garnett, and Pender (and Pettigrew during the retreat). Losses among field grade officers (majors, lieutenant colonels, and colonels) were equally appalling. And each of these officers would need to be replaced, immediately. The principal reason that there were so many casualties among officers was the fact that officers were tasked to lead from the front of their units. They also signaled to the opposing side exactly who they were—special hat, distinctive uniform, sword held high, and often riding on a horse.[26]

Lee had been facing the problem of succession even before he took over the Army of Northern Virginia. Once in the army's leadership post, the problem became acute, possibly reaching its crescendo in the loss of Stonewall Jackson just weeks before Gettysburg.

Stonewall Jackson, a confirmed micro-manager, told his subordinates basically nothing of his methods or plans, expecting blind obedience. When he was killed scouting his lines in the gathering dusk at Chancellorsville, Dick Ewell and A. P. Hill were put in his place, his II Corps being divided into two. Both of these generals were assigned largely due to seniority, not because there was any evidence that either would perform admirably in the corps commander role. Both had been very good division commanders, but that is a different matter. Division commanders work under the direction of corps commanders. Corps commanders, especially Lee's corps commanders, were expected to use a great deal of discretion, once Lee had issued the overall plan.

With only a few days' notice, they were then tasked with helping conduct the largest battle ever fought on the American continent. Were these two generals well prepared? How would they perform under the direct command of Lee? Lee's modus operandi of giving a great deal of discretion

---

[26] An interesting side note occurred on the first day of battle. On that day, as Robert Rodes led his division onto Oak Hill to attack the Federals in their right flank, he tasked his two weakest led brigades to lead the attack (and that without any appropriate reconnaissance to determine what lay before him). Because of a misunderstanding, Robert O'Neal (one brigade commander) used only three of his four regiments and he attacked on a narrow front at a place different from where Rodes had carefully indicated. Although the two brigades were meant to attack in support of each other, there was confusion about who was supposed to move first. O'Neal's ineffective attack was repulsed, leaving Alfred Iverson's (the other brigade commander) flank exposed. But the most significant problem was that the two brigade commanders chose not to lead their brigades in person, remaining behind their advance. After the battle, there were rumors among the North Carolinians that Iverson was too drunk to lead, but his battle report indicated that he deliberately chose to remain behind and historians present no evidence that alcohol was involved in his decision.

to his subordinates was in direct opposition to Jackson's micro-managing style of leadership. And both Hill and Ewell had served under Jackson.

Lee's method of leadership was on display as evening approached on the first day of the battle. He said to Dick Ewell, pointing to Cemetery Hill where Union troops were frantically digging in and placing cannon, "Take that hill, if practicable." If practicable. What did that mean? Ewell would have to use discretion. Stonewall Jackson would have simply and clearly said, "Take that hill." End of message. No room for discretion. Just follow orders. Get it done.

On the other side of the line was George Meade. He had not been prepared in any appreciable way to lead an army of a hundred thousand men. He'd moved up the ranks to corps command, where he'd performed adequately. But that's eight thousand men to coordinate. Then he took over the reins of command with five to ten times the number of men George Washington ever commanded. Meade didn't even know where the other corps were located. And now the future of the nation was placed in his hands. He must beat the Confederate general who, by reputation, was seen as nothing short of a wizard on the battlefield. At the end of the battle, he would experience the death of one corps commander (Reynolds of the I Corps) and one that was severely wounded and out of action for the rest of the war (Sickles of the III Corps) and another who was severely wounded and out of action for a protracted period (Winfield Hancock of the II Corps). Added to this was, like Lee, the loss of the incalculable talents, skills, and experience of numerous officers throughout the ranks.

Both Lee and Meade faced monumental challenges in replacing the leadership lost in and around the hamlet of Gettysburg. But before we look at talent management, and succession planning that is so critical to the success of the organization, let's first consider several aspects of the organization that must be in place in order for talent to be successfully managed.

Five Qualities of a Transformational Organization

Hopefully, by this point in the book, you have a grasp of the type of leader who will be most successful. This is the leader who is well-defined as a person, thus presenting a non-anxious presence to his colleagues. He is able to build trust because he is congruent—what he says matches how he behaves. And his leadership is molded to meet the demands of any particular situation—he may be the technical expert, he may be the synthesizing strategist peering into the future, or he may be the facilitating transformational leader, noting the competing values that constantly confront the organization.

Let's take a moment to note several aspects of the organization that this successful leader creates and/or maintains. This is the environment that will most successfully develop the people and raise up the next generation of leadership. Ron Heifetz and Marty Linsky detail five qualities of the transformational organization that need to be understood in order to lead a world-class organization in an ever-changing world, qualities that are critical to the selection, retention, and advancement of future leaders:[27]

- Responsibility for the organization's future is shared (and overrides departmental loyalties). People have a natural tendency to default to their workgroups while ignoring the larger organization. In the successful transformational organization, the leader is able to mold the leadership into a collective that is able to take responsibility for the organization as a whole, even when collective decisions come in direct contradiction to the needs and wishes of each individual leader's particular work groups.

  To what extent do people in your organization act from the perspective of the betterment of the whole, rather than their own particular department?

---

[27]   Ron Heifetz and Marty Linsky: *The Practice of Transformational Leadership*

- "Elephants in the room" are named. It is fascinating how problems within any organization, beginning with the family, are ignored, even when they exist in plain sight. The anticipation of confronting these issues creates a great deal of anxiety as to the potential consequences of that confrontation. Therefore, these issues—the resolution of which are critical to ongoing smooth functioning—lie hidden in plain sight, while everyone goes about their business pretending they're not there.

  How long does it take for problems to get from people's heads, to the water cooler, to the leadership meeting? How quickly are problems identified and discussed? Is there support to speak the unspeakable, or are people marginalized when they speak up?

- Independent judgment is expected. This goes hand in hand with the shared responsibility mentioned in our first bullet point. In a healthy organization, where talent is identified and developing, people are encouraged to exercise independent judgment. As Edwin Friedman stated in his book, *A Failure of Nerve*, the capacity to be decisive is more important than being as informed as possible. Remember, however, the previous chapter. This behavior may be encouraged verbally, but countermanded in real-time behavior, as anxiety rises around anticipated potential consequences of empowering employees.

  To what extent are people valued for offering their own perspective rather than figuring out the boss's preference and then perpetually agreeing with him? When someone takes a risk to further the mission, and it doesn't work out, to what extent is that seen as learning rather than personal failure?

- Leadership capacity is developed. Leadership is understood as an activity that needs to be taught and encouraged at all levels of the organization. This is arguably the key element in succession planning. It is not reserved for those in the C suite or those who have been identified as possessing certain innate qualities that are cherished historically in leadership manuals (but which are rarely proven consistently to embody effective leadership).

To what extent do people know where they stand in the organization and their potential for advancement? Do they have an agreed-upon plan to achieve their potential? To what extent is senior management identifying and mentoring successors?

- Reflection and continuous learning are institutionalized. Leaders within the organization are encouraged to be in a mode of continuous learning, realizing that the nature of life that surrounds us is continually changing, requiring ongoing adaption to a new world.

    Do you carve out time for reflection and learning from past experiences? How much time, space, and resources are intentionally dedicated to getting diverse input on how you could do things better or differently?

Creating an organizational culture where leadership is distributed, potential future leaders are identified and developed is critical to an organization's ongoing success. Let's turn now to how talent, as the most critical asset an organization possesses, is discovered and nurtured.

Talent Management

If you have been successful at creating the transformational organization as noted above, you will want to retain top performers in order to build and sustain this top performing organization. Though critical to the ongoing health of any organization, this is not an easy process. First, the leader must identify who are the best performers to bring into the organization. Next, he must get them in the right seats where they can perform optimally. Then, they must be continuously developed while he identifies who might be the next generation of leadership for the organization. And finally, everyone in the organization must be developed in the direction of best practices.

Notice that succession planning is embedded in an unfolding intentional program of talent management. Talent management is a process whereby superior employees are recruited; their knowledge, skills, and abilities are developed; and future leaders are identified. And all employees are prepared for advancement or promotion into ever more challenging roles, whether that be leadership roles, or ever more complex technical responsibilities. Actively engaging talent management ensures that employees are constantly developed to fill each needed role. As the organization expands, loses key employees, provides promotional opportunities, and grows, proper talent management guarantees that you have a pool of employees on hand ready and waiting to fill new roles.

Talent management actually encompasses the entire life cycle of the employee. Let's look at five important elements of that management:

- Selecting your people
- Setting expectations for your people
- Motivating your people
- Developing your people
- Succession planning for the future of your people

Remember, talent within an organization is arguably the most important resource any particular organization contains. As with any valuable resource, careful and proper management is critical to the ongoing success of that organization. And yet, too few organizations in the public, private, and not-for-profit sector seem to realize how critical this one component is to their ongoing success.

In managing the talent within any organization, leadership must constantly know whether they have the right people, who are moving at the right pace into the right positions at the right time. An effective overall talent management strategy that takes into consideration all of the elements of the above list will help paint a more promising future for organizations and for their employees.

Selecting your people. We live in an age where hiring and retaining the right people is absolutely critical to sustainable success. Two prominent examples—Google and Microsoft—demonstrate the critical importance of getting the right people on board, retaining them, and moving the right ones into leadership positions.

We often give lip service to the above idea, but then go about making mistake after mistake in the hiring process, without looking more diligently into why we are failing in this most critical area.

As we have said, most of what is truly important to us is occurring under the surface, and out of awareness to us, unless we are truly vigilant and take the time to be self-aware and understand ourselves (the well-defined leader).

Our tendency is to move away from the anxiety-provoking people/situations. Therefore, we move toward people/situations that lower our anxiety. And herein lies one key problem. When it comes to selecting people to be on our team, then to succeed us and lead us toward our desired future, we are unconsciously drawn to those who lower our anxiety. And who are those people who lower our anxiety? The people whom we most understand, who are the most predictable to us. And who are those people? Those who tend to be most *like* us. Keep in mind those who are most like us may not be the best candidates to backfill us or to serve on our teams for that matter.

This is the problem with those on a team who speak up and point out the "elephant in the room." Often these people are extremely useful to a team. But because they raise the anxiety level, they are often marginalized or altogether dismissed. This is also the problem when you are very technical, looking at a very creative person; when you are very extroverted, looking at a very introverted person; and when you are an immediate action person, looking at a deep thinker person.

Then we cover up the whole intriguing selection process with logic. Remember what we said about cognitive dissonance back in chapter 3. Our brains become anxious when we are incongruent—

saying one thing and doing another. Again, we can't exist for long with all of that anxiety. So our minds set about cleaning up the mess. And here is how it's done:

- *Self-deception.* By the systematic management of my attention, I pay attention to those issues that confirm my prejudices. I ignore evidence that goes contrary to what I believe. Or I give inordinate attention to disproving material, in order to creatively discount it.
- *Procrastination.* Contrary ideas and beliefs have a nice habit of disappearing if we put off acting on them. And of course, our anxiety recedes, which is exactly what we wanted all along.
- *Perspective switching.* There can be a number of differing perspectives on an action—our motives, intentions, what really happened. We can adopt another perspective when the perspective on what we've done proves more uncomfortable and anxiety provoking than we can handle.
- *Rationalization.* Our rational minds are expert at constructing explanations of our behavior. The fact that these explanations don't necessarily square with the truth is irrelevant. We're protected because we have an "airtight" case.
- *Group think.* We surround ourselves with people who agree with us—nothing better to lower anxiety than to surround myself with people who always agree and never challenge us.
- *Confirmation bias* is a concept every leader should have indelibly seared into their brains. It is the tendency to search for, interpret, favor, and recall information in a way that confirms one's beliefs. We utilize it when we gather or remember information selectively, or when they interpret it in a biased way. We also employ it when we interpret ambiguous evidence as supporting our existing position.

Leaders are often blinded by their own biases when it comes to hiring and then succession planning. Arguably, values and performance should be the only criteria for selection and promotion. All too often the leader is merely gazing into the mirror and selecting those who share his profile (a profile that has flaws and weaknesses, as all profiles do). Research indicates that the most valid practices for assessment are those that involve multiple methods and especially multiple raters.

Remember though, it's the people who often raise our anxiety that we need in our lives—those clashing personalities and talents that round us out, give us the bad news, contradict us, and act completely different than we would have.

So in saying all of this, we sound a note of caution. The very people that you might land on as the perfect candidates to fill positions and to succeed you could quite possibly be the worst possible candidates to move the organization forward effectively.

How do we manage our talent in such a way as to identify, retain, and develop our next generation of leadership so that we get the right people on the bus in the first place, then manage our "bench" so that it is strong when we need to fill positions that come available?

Identifying potential hires. So who are those people we first want on board in our organizations? And then how do we identify those with the potential to assume greater responsibility in the organization? Be careful here. Remember what we said about evaluation of talent? It's largely done out of awareness, "by the seat of our pants," and more often than not we get it wrong.

The Google organization takes a lot of time and thought to the hiring process. Laszlo Bock states in his book about the organization, *Work Rules! Insights from Inside Google that Will Transform How You Live and Lead*, that it is easier to get into Harvard, then into the employed ranks of Google. One interesting insight into the hiring process is that it first recognizes the extreme bias that is present in all hiring. As interviews talk with prospective hires, decisions are made unconsciously within the first few seconds. And these decisions have *nothing* to do with the competence and abilities of the potential hire to perform the job adequately. There are numerous steps and criteria that are followed by those making hiring decisions. One that stands out is hiring decisions are never placed in the hands of one person. Having one person make the decision invites bias.

Lee had a propensity for selecting fellow Virginians to assume key command positions in his Army of Northern Virginia. This led to a great deal of resentment among non-Virginians, as would be expected. It also led to marginal competence in key command positions (Dick Ewell and A. P. Hill at Gettysburg are prominent examples). We have seen this similar favoritism in family-run businesses. Children of the founder-owners are often slated to take control of the company when they have few if any competencies to lead. Their main qualification is their last name. This often proves disastrous.

My friend and business partner Ken Tucker has developed a process for hiring that seeks to cut through the biases and bad practices of hiring that so often plague the process. He has called this the idmatch© process. Beyond a candidate's resume, there are specific traits needed for an individual to be the right fit and perform optimally in a specific role. The idmatch© process allows you to identify that right hire by doing the following:

1. Identifying the critical outcomes, achievement emotions, and critical activities of the position to be filled
2. Developing questions that identify the candidate's unique difference
3. Assessing the match between each candidate's unique difference and the critical activities of specific roles
4. Assessing the match between each candidate's unique difference and the unique difference of the supervisor and peers for that specific role
5. Assessing the match between each candidate's unique difference and the culture of the organization
6. Teaching interviewers how to use the developed questions
7. Certifying each interviewer's accuracy level at a ninety-five percent rate

8. Unpacking the hiring interview and discussing with hiring manager/supervisor the likely impact of the person on the workgroup, workflow, and team performance

9. Providing insight on how to best motivate, develop, and position the new hire

10. Developing metrics for the new hire's performance, to be assessed and reviewed six months into the job

Setting expectations for your people. An essential part of leadership is being clear with your team about expectations. Did you know that fewer than fifty percent of employees claim they know what is expected of them at work? That's an amazing statistic! Several points are critical here:

- Define the *right outcomes.* Don't dictate how work should be done! There is no such thing as a "best way" to do anything. Your first instinct must be to trust the people you've selected, and let them, in their own uniqueness, get to the outcomes you have clearly delineated with them.
- Define how each employee will contribute to those outcomes.
- Communicate those expectations continually. Meet with employees four or five times a year to check progress, offer advice, and agree on course corrections.

Having said that, *never* force all of your team to follow the same path to those outcomes. That's a huge mistake managers constantly make. Each person must find his/her own path to the desired outcome.

Motivating your people. Your job as a leader is to turn your people's strengths and talents into performance. To do this, you must focus on people's strengths. In other words, you must let them become more of who they already are. That goes contrary to most management thinking that says identify the weaknesses, then coach them, threaten them, send them to workshops, whatever, to make sure they overcome their weaknesses. You must manage around each person's weakness and get to their strengths, where the true power lies.

You are charged with other responsibilities, but your managing succeeds or fails based on your ability to make employees more productive working with you rather than with someone else. To pull this off, employees must genuinely believe that their success is your primary goal. The employee will give her all only when she feels supported, challenged, understood, and stretched to be as successful as her talents allow.

By the way, an important adage (which is also counterintuitive) is to spend most of your time with your best people. There's no use in spending all of your energy on nonperformers or low performers. To the best of your ability, you need to get those folks into more productive jobs, if that's possible. Pay attention to the behaviors of your superstars.[28]

There are several things to consider about poor performers. First, are your poor performers motivated? If the answer is no, try whatever means there are in your power to get them "off the bus." If they are motivated, but not doing well, I'd think, "Is this person on the right seat on the bus?" So many people in the workforce are miscast, placed into jobs that are not fulfilling or not utilizing their strengths, rather than energizing and calling forth their true strengths and potential.

And that's important for all your people. Discover what is unique about each person and capitalize on it. Get them in the right seats to begin with, and notice the acceleration in performance.

Another reality to consider is that what makes one person feel appreciated does not make another person feel appreciated. Research indicates that employees favor recognition from managers and supervisors by a margin of 2–1 over recognition from coworkers. However, most of us would agree that if we feel appreciated by our coworkers, life is much more pleasant.[29]

---

[28] Marcus Buckingham discusses many of these counterintuitive management rules in his book, *First, Break All the Rules.*

[29] Paul White and Gary Chapman, *The 5 Languages of Appreciation in the Workplace*

It should be noted that people have different "languages" of appreciation. Some prefer words of affirmation, others need quality time spent with them, others need to see acts of service done for them, and still others prefer tangible gifts. Unfortunately, people tend to give to people the acts of appreciation that they themselves prefer, which are much less effective than supplying what each individual actually prefers.

Improving employee commitment and retention. So how do we retain those most valuable employees? Many quickly answer this question with, "Well, just pay them more." But money is rarely a top motivator as employees decide to stay or leave an organization. Let's look at some of the factors that are critical in retention:

- *Creating the right culture.* Certain cultures retain top performers; others repel them. Low employee morale, usually pointing to a lack of trust in leadership, poor employee-manager relationships, or many other issues have been discussed previously. A lack of satisfaction and commitment to the organization usually causes an employee to withdraw and begin looking for other opportunities. Pay so often does not play as large a role in inducing turnover as is typically believed.

- Remember what we said in chapter 4: people want to affiliate with those organizations that have compelling codes that contain a mission around which each employee can align.

- *Getting in the right seat.* First, getting employees in the right "seats" is critical. Note above how Ken Tucker has developed procedures for identifying exactly what the right seat is for each employee.

- People perform at the top precisely because they are operating within their ID. Their jobs energize them. Unfortunately, so often their reward for top performance is to place them in positions where their ID is much less utilized, such as a top engineer being placed in management. Engineering and management bear no skill set correspondence. So by doing this, the employee is immediately placed in a situation where their performance will suffer, their energy at work will diminish, and the possibility of losing this person increases.

Developing your people, especially potential leaders. It should be noted that new employees consistently place continuous professional development at or near the top of their criteria for choosing an employer. Once potential leaders have been identified, either outside or within the organization, these people need to be developed. And the first thing so many organizations think is, "Let's send all of those potential leaders off to training." The amount of money spent by organizations for training each year is staggering. And much if not most of it is marginally useful.

So what to do? Maybe just allow people to pile up experience until they're ready to assume leadership positions. Research into people becoming outstanding in what they do is discouraging. It suggests that no matter how long people continue in their areas of employment, they fail to get any better at doing what they've done, and in fact, some people actually get *worse* with experience. It also suggests that people with lots of experience in a particular job are no better than those with little experience.

This is not good news when we consider that individuals and companies must continue to kick up their performance in order to compete in our ever-changing world. In fact, in this world community with increasingly interconnected economies, people now find themselves competing with the world's best. So what are we to do? Geoff Colvin details several helpful points:[30]

Find ways to develop people within their jobs. A challenge is often how to develop people without necessarily constantly moving them to new jobs. Eli Lilly has established a program where employees don't leave their jobs, but take on additional work assignments to

---

[30]   Geoff Colvin, *Talent Is Overrated* (New York: Portfolio, 2008), p. 129 ff.

expand their expertise. The Federal Aviation Administration (and other federal agencies) will allow people to go on details to other parts of the organization for limited amounts of time for the same purpose.

Encourage leaders to be active in their communities. This strategy actually has two benefits. We have found that organizations that build healthy world-class organizations are able to develop into good citizens within their communities. And encouraging leaders to be more involved is a way to increase this good citizen profile. Secondly, leaders who are active within their communities also have the opportunity to further develop their leadership skills and capacity.

Succession planning for the future of your people. The Civil War had by the summer of 1863 been raging for over two years. Armies had grown from a few thousand to now tens of thousands. Leaders at first had found commissions by virtue of their abilities to recruit, to organize and drill, and their political connections at home and in Washington. After two years of fighting, it had become apparent who had the necessary qualities of leadership to command regiments, battalions, brigades, corps, and armies.

Because senior officers tended to lead from the front, casualties among their ranks had been appalling, necessitating their immediate replacement. Many of the subsequent appointments proved exemplary. Others performed passably well. Often the replacing officers were questionable and performed poorly. It behooved the commanders in both armies to, among other pressing duties, keep an eye on potential talent, for in the heat of battle, new leadership would need to be christened immediately.

Succession planning identifies and develops internal people with the potential to fill key leadership positions in the organization. It increases the availability of experienced and capable employees who are prepared to assume these roles as they become available.

Arguably, selection of leaders is the single most important step that is taken to either change a culture or leave the culture as is. As we have seen, leadership is the irrefutably critical element in creating and maintaining healthy organizational life. Unfortunately as we have said, organizations tend to get stuck as leaders select people much like themselves, with the same nonthreatening ideas (they're nonthreatening because they mirror my own). Rare is the leader who is constantly seeking those around her who will challenge her way of thinking.

What makes this all-important principle a difficult step, and in fact a possible threat, is the fact that this also often creates a crisis within the leader (competing internal values that we saw in chapter 7). I am actually raising up the person who will replace me, which means that I am expendable. It also might mean that the person I raise up is able in fact to do a better job than I do. And it also means that the best candidate may go against what I, the current leader, think is the most important initiative of all, and that is maintaining the status quo (because in Phase II of the S curve, all of our numbers are so good at the present time, and our stakeholders are all so happy. Why would we select a rabble-rouser to head this very successful venture?).

Keep in mind that we are not just talking about back-filling vacant positions. And unfortunately that is exactly the way many organizations go about what they consider succession—a one-off activity that must be done when people walk out the door. And often the selection defaults to seniority—"Mary has been here the longest. She deserves this position."

Remember, succession planning is a comprehensive strategy within a larger strategy of talent management that identifies, develops, and therefore maintains key top performers for the overall good and stability of the organization. It is as critical a strategy as your marketing strategy.

When a person just doesn't look like a leader. The movie *Moneyball* concerns the Oakland A's baseball team and its general manager Billy Beane. This team perennially ranks near the bottom of the salary list of major league teams. The movie explains how Beane, desperate to select good players with very little money, turns to a Yale econ major who has come up with a totally different method for player selection. The "tried and true" method over the years, the method by which

Beane himself had been selected as a player, had involved what the Yale graduate explained to be faulty statistics and subjectivity. This young man introduced a whole new way of understanding player selection, a method the old guard scouts immediately rejected. But the method proved not only effective for the A's, but now has been adopted by many if not all major league teams to a greater or lesser degree

Abraham Lincoln was a man who didn't, by all measures of leadership, appear to be in any way a leader. Tall and ungainly, unusual facial features, with clothes that never quite fit, a high-pitched voice, and a backwoods accent with stories that bordered on off color, he was not by any present standards the picture of a leader. Generally, people look to all the wrong measures when considering what might make an effective leader.

Always, always question your own evaluative abilities. That's right; question your supposed good judgment and rationality. History has proved over and over again that we are not as rational as we like to give ourselves credit for being. You might just be overlooking the very best leadership candidates that populate your organization.

The Battle

Experts have tended to disagree as to the importance of the battle of Gettysburg, whether in fact it was the turning point of the war. But what they have tended to agree on was the fact that, as Lee's army pulled out of Gettysburg in the pouring rain, it had for all intents and purposes lost its offensive capabilities. Yes, the war would continue for another twenty-one months, but Lee would never again be able to launch an offensive of any consequence. Not only had Lee lost over 25,000 men that the South could not replace, he had decimated the ranks of his leadership.

Meade also had lost 25,000 men and countless leaders. But he had a vast pool of resources in men and materiel from which he could draw going forward. Lee had understood that he could not win a protracted war, because of this disparity. This had led Lee to seek that one set piece battle that would provoke European powers to recognize the legitimacy of the Confederate cause and provide critical resources for the successful prosecution of the war (the way the French had come to the aid of the colonies during the American Revolution).

But in the week following the battle of Gettysburg, Lee would back his army up against the rain-swollen Potomac River, digging an elaborate defensive position at Williamsport, Maryland. There he would wait, as the days passed, until the swollen river receded, and he could finally evacuate his army back into Virginia.

Meade cautiously followed Lee and confronted the Confederate army in its positions against the Potomac. But Meade hesitated. Lee's defensives were formidable. Meade's army had been severely handled for three days back in Gettysburg. Meade still possessed a cautious mind. Though having fought an admirable tactical battle, he performed much like McClellan at Antietam, contenting himself to remain completely on the defensive—no aggressive spirit in evidence. And he had faced Robert E. Lee, who seemed to possess powers that defied description, even though these had not been demonstrated at Gettysburg. The official ranks of leadership back in Washington expected Meade to seize this opportunity and crush the southern army once and for all. This did not happen. The disappointment was pronounced, especially with Abraham Lincoln.

The Confederate army was allowed to slip back over the river and return to the friendly confines of Virginia where it could rest, refit, and prepare to fight another day.

Take Action Managing Your People and Raising Up the Next Generation of Leadership

- First, take a look at your organization. Answer the questions posed under each bullet point:
  - o To what extent do people in your organization act from the perspective of the betterment of the whole, rather than their silo or department?
  - o How long does it take for problems to get from people's heads, to the water cooler, to the leadership meeting?

How quickly are problems identified and discussed? Is there support to speak the unspeakable?

o To what extent are people valued for offering their own perspective rather than figuring out the boss's preference? When someone takes a risk to further the mission, and it doesn't work out, to what extent is that seen as learning rather than personal failure?

o Do you carve out time for reflection and learning from past experiences? How much time, space, and resources are intentionally dedicated to getting diverse input on how you could do things better or differently?

- Talent management encompasses the life cycle of the employee. Note each of the elements of this life cycle, and check those items which are adequately covered in your organization, and note those items that will need special attention going forward:
  o Recruiting and hiring
  o Onboarding
  o Training
  o Professional development
  o Performance management
  o Workforce planning
  o Leadership development
  o Career development
  o Cross-functional work assignments
  o Succession planning
  o Employee exit process

Chapter 9

Leading Transformationally

After the Battle

Four and a half months after the battle of Gettysburg, Lincoln took a train from Washington up to the little hamlet that was already becoming etched in the American mind. After detraining, he rode over the shattered countryside, noting the blasted woodlots, the burned houses, and the trampled crops. Here was the scene of unspeakable horrors, of seemingly senseless death and destruction, and of war in all its meaninglessness and cruelty.

Just a few short weeks before his tour, hogs had rooted poorly buried bodies out of the ground and devoured them. Indeed all of Gettysburg and the surrounding fields had been transformed into a makeshift burying ground. The whole scene following the battle had been horrific— bloated and rotting bodies were everywhere. Thousands of horses had to be quickly burned. The accouterments of war blanketed the landscape. The smell of rotting flesh was replaced by the smell of burning flesh. This macabre scene was precisely why it had been determined to create a national cemetery, a final resting place for those who had died in the struggle.

As Lincoln rode through the countryside to see for himself where this horrendous battle had been fought, he was, in his fifty-fourth year, a special figure to behold. He was tall, all of 6´4”, with stooped and rounded shoulders supporting a head bent forward and turned downward. His face exposed deep subtleties. The skin was shaded in light brown like a well-cured leather, lined and wrinkled etched from some unspoken but profound sadness. Even when he laughed, you could see it, especially in the eyes, a gloom that settled over him, overshadowing all else with the darkness. His mind often roamed in those valleys of despair.

His voice was a high-pitched tenor, but was clear and appealing when he spoke. At those rare times when he became excited, his voice would rise to a falsetto, riveting attention as each word was driven home. His language bore the lilt of the backwoods, the humorous and sometimes bawdy story covering the darkness within.

He could easily have been mistaken for a farmer. He hailed from prairies and hills, not city streets. Old style black suits, always worn wrinkled, were draped over his body. Then there was the perennial black tie. His odd contours made it near impossible to fit him with proper clothing. But there was a quiet dignity mixed with wisdom, compassion, and a deep, awkward courage.

He had no family heritage, no education, no languages beyond his backwoods-accented English, and no exposure to the great world outside his own country.

Lincoln had virtually no experience as an executive. Arguably he was the least prepared for the office of president of any chief executive we've ever had. He'd served one term in congress and a little in the state legislature. But other than that, he'd been part of a two-man law firm trudging around the state trying cases.

He is a man who was easy to underestimate, and indeed he fostered that image—the simple backwoods rail splitter. But underneath the facade was a shrewd politician, gifted in not only understanding people and the human condition but expert in swaying and often manipulating individuals and publics to his will.

As president, Lincoln had taken an oath to preserve, protect, and defend the constitution (what he was authorized to do). This duty constrained his options. "I am naturally anti-slavery. If slavery is not wrong, nothing is wrong . . . Yet I have never understood that the Presidency conferred upon me an unrestricted right to act officially on this judgment and feeling." The office (what I am authorized to do) "forbade me to practically indulge my primary abstract judgment on the moral question of slavery."

Abraham Lincoln had come to Gettysburg in November after the battle to help dedicate the new national cemetery. His address would be one of the most profound transformational statements ever made. He had considered what were the seminal points he must emphasize.

Our new nation was dedicated to the proposition that all men are created equal, versus the competing value that we have established a culture of slavery.

Can a republic—where every person and state has a say in the direction of our nation, versus national interests taking precedence over individual or state considerations—long endure? The world is watching—a world basically ruled by monarchs and despots who scoff at the possibility of a republic actually lasting.

Competing Values

For the nation, on the one hand, was the guiding principle that "all men are created equal." On the other hand, it was power and the prevailing self-interest of slavery, where slavery was a deeply entrenched institution that was central to the economic survival of the South and to a lesser degree the whole nation.

Lincoln had the deeply held conviction that slavery was a moral evil (with immense transformational/transformative implications). Yet he was a politician and had to bow to political realities that mandated his choices at key moments (what he in fact was authorized to do).

But slave ships had visited our colonial shores 250 years previously, and slavery by the mid-nineteenth century had become firmly entrenched in the economy of the nation, especially the South. What to do with these competing values—freedom and equality of opportunity competing with economic stability? These two opposing values still compete with one another.

And standing in the middle of these two opposing values was Abraham Lincoln, who would attempt to place them before the American mind and the war that had sprung from the inability to resolve this issue—Lincoln, the ultimate transformational leader.

What Lincoln understood in his warring nation was not principally tactical or strategic in nature. It was transformational. That being said, he seemed to instinctively realize that he couldn't just use the "bully pulpit" of the presidency to ram his ideas through the American mind (as the authority figure could when the issue was tactical). He'd have to place before the people the values—and by implication, the competing values—on which our republic was founded. Then he would have to oversee the conflict (not necessarily between North and South) within the North broiling over what these values actually looked like and how they should be lived out.

Jefferson Davis also faced overwhelming transformational issues. One of the most prominent of these was the issue of state rights. Southern states had left the Union over slavery, and each state's prerogative to determine how it would decide this critical question. But now there were eleven independent states who, in order to survive, needed to come together in unity and in many instances lay aside their individual state rights and sit down and determine a collective course. And therein lay the competing values—individual state rights versus the collective national need to defend itself.

Whether or not Davis understood this glaring competition between conflicting values is unclear. But this competition between the individual state and the collective Confederate nation came to a head numerous times.

Another example was the need to keep the Confederate army together. Few people, back in the spring of 1861 when the war began, understood that the war would last more than a month or two. So men were recruited into the army for a one-year enlistment (which seemed almost too long).

Then the shooting began, and it became apparent that the war was going to last. So Lee in the spring of 1862 realized that most of the army now needed to defend Richmond as Union troops marched up the Peninsula toward the city would soon melt away. He had to retain an army ready to go home. What to do? It was obvious that conscription would be the answer—a non-volunteer army of drafted soldiers. This was not welcome news either to the soldiers or to their home state governors, who saw their authority eroding as a strong central government began to mandate measures they understood were reserved for themselves (sound familiar?). These competing values were never properly navigated as the war continued, quite possibly because no one in the Confederate leadership understood the issue. Consequently, there was no "Gettysburg Address" issued from the Confederate White House laying before the people the particulars of the matter.

Another transformational issue that reared its head toward the end of the war was the possibility of recruiting slaves into the southern army. Lee seemed to understand this as transformational—these men were slaves, who had been considered sub-human. Now the nation was arming them and giving them their freedom, as if everything we'd ever thought about them was in error. But as the leadership of the Confederacy debated the issue of arming slaves, the anxiety over the implications of this measure was simply too high, and the proposition was allowed to die, even as the southern cause also died.

Gettysburg Address

The Gettysburg Address was arguably the greatest speech ever given on this continent. Possibly it is the greatest speech given in the English language (as none other than Winston Churchill stated). Remember, for Lincoln, words were his weapons. And here, and in his second inaugural address, he brought out his heavy artillery. In these two speeches, he placed before us in plain language where we came from, who we are, and who we are meant to be—what we have always valued and how we had fallen short of that ideal.

It's then not startling to realize that the greatest sermon preached during that war took a mere two and one half minutes and was preached by a politician dedicating a cemetery to the dead of Gettysburg. Lincoln was indeed the greatest "preacher" of the day. He laid out the new national gospel there at Gettysburg on the hill above the town, in the cemetery, where our troops had unlimbered their guns, and shelled the advancing Virginians and North Carolinians. He then shaped that gospel more clearly when he stood on the east front of the capitol building and uttered his second inaugural address, which summarized for future generations, not only what that war was all about but what our new national faith was all about.

It was decided by the powers that be that a proper cemetery was in order, a final resting place where the honored dead could be reburied and celebrated in the years to come. Lincoln somehow knew that it was his responsibility as the leader of the nation to mold from the shapeless mass of suffering not just a simple explanation. No. He knew he had to focus the American mind on the meaning of it all, to transform the battle into a symbol, not of senseless violence, but of national purpose and the grand ideals upon which the nation was founded.

So his little speech of 272 words was aimed neither at the battle nor at the battle's dead. It was aimed at the American mind. Like a well-aimed shot, it was designed to position this whole terrible war in a historical context, but more than that, to position the war in a moral context, to shift our values if you will, our way of seeing ourselves in our nation (not technical or strategic, but transformative).

His fundamental message, beginning with an unconscious echo of a little speech he gave on July 7, was this: the American republic was founded in 1776 around the principle of human equality, and we are now fighting a civil war which tests whether that was a sufficiently good foundation; here, we are dedicating a cemetery to those who have fallen in that war, but in fact the real dedication must be a dedication of ourselves to seeing that the war is won and that the principle is vindicated.

But more than met the eye was packed into this little address. For one thing, it was yet another opportunity for Lincoln to establish the Declaration of Independence as the moral spirit animating the constitution and to see the war as a struggle for that moral spirit, rather than merely an overgrown dispute about certain procedural niceties of the constitution. The opening line "Four score and seven years ago, our Fathers brought forth on this continent a new nation, conceived in liberty and dedicated to the proposition that all men are created equal" fixed at one stroke the foundations of the republic in 1776, not 1789 (when the con-

stitution went into effect), and around a moral principle, not a question of process.

Yet, at the same time, this was not the dedication of a moral fanatic, like John Brown. The equality to which the republic was dedicated was a proposition, which was something very different indeed from what Thomas Jefferson had intended when he spoke of the equality of "all men" as the first of a series of "self-evident truths." "Equality," then, was a proposition, like one of the Euclidean theorems he had worked his way through in the 1850s, to be demonstrated and defended by reason rather than accepted as the voice of an instinctive common moral sense.

Technical vs. Transformational (Transformational) Issues

You might now be thinking to yourself, *I'll never give a Gettysburg Address where I place before the nation the compelling competing values that face her.* No, probably not. But as you lead (and by the way, parenting is a principal form of leadership, as is housecleaning, auto mechanics, etc.), you will be faced with situations that are not primarily tactical (technical) or strategic, but transformational.

Technical problems, as we stated earlier, are those that can be solved with expertise. They do not involve competing loyalties or behaviors that flow from competing values. Transformational challenges, on the other hand, are those challenges that represent competing loyalties, conflicted values, usually leading to systemic dysfunction.

Why systemic dysfunction? Because of misalignment (as we continually underline). An organization, be it a family, government agency, club, place of worship, or multinational corporation, confronts competing values continually. Unrecognized, these competing values can easily turn into incongruence and misalignment.

1. For Lincoln, the misalignment was in a nation around the value of equality for all versus slavery for some.
2. For parents, the misalignment might be with a father or mother talking about how critical family time together

is versus working longer hours to make ends meet (ends which often don't meet because of overspending on nonessentials).

3. For a faith-based organization, misalignment concerning reaching out to the poor and marginalized in the community versus maintaining a tidy upper-middle-class venue (which happens to pay the bills).

4. For a corporation, misalignment between staying on the cutting edge with large allocations to R&D versus keeping an efficient organization running smoothly in the near term relying on yesterday's products to satisfy the bottom line and shareholders.

Notice that often one of the competing values is economic. "We said we believe in this, but then the economic realities set in, and we've had to radically alter our program." That was the essential problem with slavery. We said that all are equal, but economic realities, mainly in the South but also in the North, demanded the perpetuation of slavery.

When the issue is transformational, expertise is irrelevant. That's because the issues are related to values, behaviors, and attitudes. As a result, the problem does not lend itself to easy definition, but requires further inquiry and learning. The technical authority asks, "What's the problem?" The transformational leader asks, "What's the question?"

Transformational issues are often hard to identify clearly, require changing hearts and minds, and often are championed by someone who cares but may not have the authority to effect change. When transformational issues are involved, people have to learn new ways and must choose among what appear to be contradictory values. Technical issues can be *managed*, not so with transformational challenges. Let's look at how transformational challenges actually work.

One example of this is a cardiologist, who posed this scenario to one of my business partners. He said that he'd have a person come in to see him. The doctor would perform bypass surgery (he was the technical expert). But the doctor then said to my partner, "I can do the surgery and solve the immediate problem. But I know that if the patient doesn't make significant changes in his life style (losing weight, exercise, generally more balanced living), he would be back in my office for the same procedure in five years, or he'd be dead." What to do? The doctor's expertise no longer applied. He'd have to see this issue as transformational, and thus solvable, or at least navigable by the stakeholders, in this case the patient and his family and close community.[31]

Transformational Challenges

Two transformational challenges bear noting:

1. *The gap between espoused values and the way people are actually behaving.* Transformational issues lurk in the gap between what we say is important to us (e.g., "It's important to spend time with my family") and what we actually do (I spend eighty hours a week at work). Individuals and organizations both develop gaps between what they say is important (stated values) and how they actually make decisions and behave (operating values). This leads to erosion of trust as people act incongruently (noted earlier). Transformational issues always require a deeper level of change, going to the core of what people value and believe, requiring modifying established habits and patterns of behavior.

---

[31] In this case, the doctor was directed to have the patient bring in his extended network of relationships—spouse, children, siblings, and employer. The doctor was then directed to tell the assemblage, "John here has just had bypass surgery. It was successful, but he will have one of two things happen in the next five years if he does not significantly alter his lifestyle (eating, exercise, etc.). He will be back in my office for more surgery, or he will be dead. So you as his significant community must discuss this, for the alternatives will radically affect you."

What makes this even more difficult is the fact that people tend to be overconfident in their ability to make proper moral judgments, ignoring evidence to the contrary. This tendency is most evident when two things are in play: the situation is high pressure, and the situation is inherently morally ambiguous. What made the years leading up to the Civil War confusing and ambiguous was the fact that slavery had been written into the constitution and was then backed up by numerous state and local laws. Yes, there were the values of "all men are created equal" competing with state-sponsored slavery. But how could each individual decide for himself or herself what was the proper course of action?

War had broken out precisely because the nation to that point had been completely unable to resolve these competing values—protecting the freedom and equality of all peoples versus slavery was deeply embedded in the economic fabric of the South (and to a lesser degree in the North), and to give these enslaved people their freedom would be to wreak economic ruin on the South.

Many actions today (reference Enron and their shadowy financial practices) meet the letter of the law, at least as smart attorneys can intuit the meaning, but ignore its spirit. Often organizations incentivize behaviors that increase the bottom line, while dancing very close to the edge of acceptable moral behavior.

2. *Competing commitments.* Individuals and organizations both have many commitments. Unfortunately, these commitments often come into conflict one with the other. And when one commitment must be chosen over another, people will experience losses. There is no win-win. If what you are committed to wins, what I'm committed to loses.

The southern people had to wrestle with their commitment to slavery and the need to free the slaves in order for them to fight for the South. They also had to wrestle with their commitment to state rights and their need to come together as a collective nation, sacrificing certain individual prerogatives to collectively fight a war.

As a parent/employee, you probably have to wrestle between standing on the sidelines of your child's soccer game and staying late at the office so you can get ahead and achieve your career goals. And you've probably told yourself that *my career goals will in fact enhance my family goals.* But that might just be a rationalization you've told yourself.

There are signs that transformational issues might be lurking.
We've been asked repeatedly by leaders for the signs that would let us know that transformational issues are at hand. Be advised also that there are probably no issues that are purely transformational. Issues have a way of blending the technical with the transformational. That's what usually makes it easy to focus on the technical elements. They're often much easier to spot, and rounding up an expert to solve them is a much simpler proposition. But when a technical solution is applied to an issue that has a lot of transformational elements embedded, that technical solution more often than not will itself become a problem.

You have a cycle of failure. You've tried one thing after another (all technical), and the problem persists. Look at the slavery issue once again. When the constitution was crafted in Philadelphia in 1787, a provision for slavery was included as a compromise between the slave-holding South and the North (who also participated in the slave trade and profited handsomely from it, though not itself needing the services of slaves). These technical compromises (technical fixes) continued for the next eighty-five years as southern and northern politicians attempted to "solve" the problem. Finally, the country broke apart and exploded into civil war, the technical fixes being wholly inadequate to solve the problem.

Dependence on authority. People in your organization keep turning to you, or other authorities, to solve the problems. People both

North and South, abolitionists and slaveholders, all turned to their politicians to "solve" the problem of slavery. The politicians applied technical compromise after technical compromise, all to no avail. The problem ran deep within each individual American and his/her core values. Arguably each citizen would have to wrestle with the transformational issue: we're a free and equal society versus our economic need to hold certain people in bondage.

Complaints are increasingly used to describe the current situation. There is no problem-solving occurring, merely the sound of complaints and whining. This situation characterizes the years immediately preceding the Civil War. In fact, the last five presidents before Lincoln proved more or less inept with helping the American people wrestle with the transformational issues that were at stake. Whining turned to warring, as people saw guns as the only way (and again a technical solution) to solving the problem. Let's look at some of the forms that complaining can take as people are unable to understand, much less confront, transformational issues.

Speaking the unspeakable. Whenever people in organizations get together to discuss issues, there are actually two conversations occurring: one is heard in public, while the other goes on in people's heads. There's the public conversation and the private in-the-head conversation. There's also the conversation that occurs after the public conversation, around the water cooler. In fact, the more dangerous certain topics are to discuss in public, the more protracted will be the private conversations. However, if an organization wants to move forward, it simply must allow these unspeakable conversations to surface and be discussed openly.

Distracting. Jokes, misdirected comments, denial of the problem, and focusing on the technical aspects of the problem go a long way in diverting attention from what is truly important.

Blaming. Scapegoating and marginalizing people also allow the true nature of the transformational problem to be avoided.

Rounding up the usual suspects to solve the problem hasn't worked. If the authorities can't solve it, bring in the technical experts to dicker with it. This happens over and over in congress, both before the Civil

War and today. There are gnawing issues that the American people face today, many of which have major transformational implications, with technical experts being rallied in an attempt to solve them. The most glaring is immigration. We're a nation of immigrants (one value). But allowing unrestrained immigration taxes the very core of national stability (another value). Each of us as stakeholders must wrestle with the implications of this conflict.

Increasing conflict. Because nothing's worked, we'll fight among ourselves about who's to blame for this. As Lincoln said in his second inaugural speech, "And the war came."

For each of us, as we consider the persistent problems that plague our organizations, it might be prudent to consider the above signs to see if transformational issues might be lurking under the surface. If so, our leadership will have to alter from the technical authority to the transformational leader.

Who Is the Transformational Leader?

Hopefully you're getting the idea that transformational leadership is different from the profile of a leader that is usually presented. Transformational leadership is difficult work, difficult because it involves helping individuals make hard value choices and difficult because it challenges what people hold dear and thereby generates resistance from many of those affected. When people resist transformational work, their first goal is to preserve what they have, and that means shutting down those advocating leading the change. The issue of slavery is just such a transformational issue that challenged people. The competing values were obvious (all men are equal versus economic stability). The losses for many were pronounced (my way of life and society's economic stability). They moved to shut down those advocating abolition (they seceded and began the Civil War).

When fears and passions run high, people can become desperate as they look to authorities for answers. People rarely elect or hire anyone to disturb their jobs or their lives. People expect leaders to use their authority to provide them with the right answers that will keep the status quo in place, not to confront them with disturbing questions and difficult choices. When people look to authorities for easy answers to transformational challenges, they end up with dysfunction. They expect the person in charge to know what to do, and under the weight of that responsibility, those in authority frequently end up spouting technical fixes (as if the issue could be fixed with a simple solution) or disappointing people, or they get spit out of the system in the belief that a new "leader" will solve the problem.

Solutions are also not clear. In fact, transformational issues are rarely if ever solved, they are *navigated.*

Leadership (the Verb)

When people think of great leaders of the past, they usually assume that there are several immutable traits, basically inborn, that define those who lead. I'd like to propose that leadership is better understood as a verb. And this is for several reasons. First, if it's a verb, then basically anyone can exercise it, not a chosen few. Second, a verb defines action, and action, more than anything else, defines leadership. A verb also connects a subject with its object, and leadership is the engagement of people in the critical issues requiring transformational change. Leadership as a verb connects people and problems in the active context of stepping up to the plate.

Unlike a noun, a verb is never static. Its work never ends. Leading transformational change is an ongoing quest with no guarantees of ever getting "there." Leadership as a verb is not about the leader who makes the decisions. In organizations, leadership is about the leader's activity of mobilizing others to do the hard work of change.

Finally, most importantly, a verb is energy. Transformational leadership requires endless energy. The work of rooting out deep cultural dysfunctions is ongoing and painful work.

What Does the Transformational Leader Do?
Critical Leadership Behaviors[32]

More often than we realize, systems cause their own crises. That's hard for us to see, because we tend to blame external forces or the mistakes of individuals. We look for scapegoats. We blame others. We sometimes blame ourselves. But, in fact, we are all caught up in a complex interworking of dynamics that shape our behavior more than we would care to admit. Note these points:

- Today's problems come from yesterday's "solutions." What worked in the past does not work anymore because of a change in the competitive landscape.
- The harder you push, the harder the system pushes back. The system is an unforgiving thing. It can't be defeated, only understood and, over time, transformed.
- Faster often results in slower. It's difficult to overestimate the importance of critical reflection and building ownership of stakeholders on the front end of a change initiative.
- Small changes can produce big results—but the areas of greatest leverage are often the least obvious.
- There is no one to blame. We tend to want to make people scapegoats and culprits. But in fact people generally behave exactly how the system rewards them for behaving.
- Crisis and sabotage can be signs of success.

Notice each of these issues is counterintuitive. And that's what makes organizational life challenging. Marcus Buckingham wrote a book, *First, Break All the Rules,* that details all of the management issues that are likewise counterintuitive.

Often our worse enemy is our past success. We get trapped into doing things that have always worked in the past, even if those

---

[32]   From Ron Heifetz and Marty Linsky, *The Practice of Transformational Leadership*

once-valid approaches are not the most effective anymore. This was especially true of Lee at Gettysburg. He had two things working against him in his past successes: First, he thought his men invincible. Second, following the successful battle plan at Chancellorsville, he thought the same plan would work at Gettysburg (hit them on the flank first, then follow-up with a blow through the middle.).

We all have default ways of behaving, thinking, and leading. Our "defaults" are comfortable for us largely because they have worked in the past. But the downside of defaults is that they blind us to a more robust and wider array of solutions that could actually create more value.

Let's turn to the specific behaviors that each leader must employ in order to maintain alignment.

Observing: getting on the balcony. This may be the most important function of leadership (we already touched on this in chapter 3). Everyone knows that the "fog of war," whether real combat or the warfare that swirls around each of us from time to time in our organizational lives, can blur our ability to reflect on what is occurring and what is truly important at any given moment. Great athletes have the ability to play the game while maintaining a detached ability to observe the unfolding drama as a whole. Wayne Getzky's (former NHL hockey great) quotation "I skate to where the puck is going to be" is an example of this.

It's far easier, especially when intensity rises, to adopt established beliefs, or the group think (consensus building) of the moment, than to critically evaluate the merits of a situation. The herd instinct makes it hard to see another direction when there is so much dust obscuring the scene.

Getting on the balcony, and making observations from there, is arguably the critical first step in exercising leadership. This is not a disengaged position. Absenting oneself from the fray, even for a moment, can be very difficult, but yields important perspectives. I remove myself from the immediate conundrum to take a position that allows me to get a better handle on how all the processes are unfolding and conspiring to create the challenge.

However, getting on the balcony does require:

- The leader to be well defined and non-anxious (blue zone = "None of what I'm seeing is personal to me"). Members of the organization are often consumed with anxiety and demand immediate action from the leader. This sense of urgency can tap directly into the leader's own personal issues ("I must be competent. Therefore I must rescue these people with a technical solution").
- This allows him to remain resolute when the temptation and seduction are to be drawn into the action and lose the critical perspective. Getting people to address those deeply felt issues is dangerous and risky. It is always easier to jump into the fray, follow the "party line," and attempt to rescue those who are most anxious.

Once on the balcony:

- You can hear individual stories, while listening to the "music" under those stories that will give you critical information as to where a person is actually coming from; how they defend their actions, habits, and ways of thinking; and how they go about resisting the difficult value choices and changes that are critical.
- You can see the vital interactions and relationships that make up the interlocking systems within your organization.
  - ✓ Find out where people are, who relates to whom, how, who takes center stage, who is marginalized (and therefore their voice is never heard), etc.
  - ✓ Where have coalitions formed that may or may not be useful to the overall goals of the organization?

But to actually effect change, the leader must come off the balcony and once again "enter the dance." As the leader is able to see emerging patterns of relationship, he is able to adjust his behavior accordingly.

But a word of caution, the leader must also avoid making snap judgments and voicing those "balcony" observations immediately. Reality is many-faceted and can prove elusive to even the most careful observation. This is especially important when judging another person's intentions. When I make a snap decision about another person's intentions, almost invariably I have projected my own issues onto the person I'm evaluating.

Interpreting. Once you come down from the balcony, you must interpret to your people what you observe to be happening. Organizations want you to accept their interpretation of reality. Your job is to reframe toward an alternate view of reality (which is also to move your people toward the mission). People caught up in the moment of crisis rarely are able to see clearly the processes around them.

In battle, generals are constantly trying to get a grasp of the situation. Civil War battlefields were notorious for smoke, ear-splitting noise, and general confusion. The terrain of the eastern United States includes very little flat ground for easy observation and maneuver. Mountains, valleys, gorges, basins, and hillocks punctuated by forests, rock outcroppings, and woodlots abounded. On a windless day, smoke would become trapped in defiles and dells at key points on the battlefield, concealing whole regiments from their commanders and the enemy. This was especially true on terrains like those experienced at Antietam Creek where whole regiments and brigades disappeared in the undulating, smoke-shrouded countryside.

The questions that perpetually arose at Gettysburg for the commanders directing the action there, and for leaders of all organizations (beginning with parents in families), are as follows: What is the actual situation? What is the reality that now confronts my organization? Until these questions are successfully answered (and remember, our minds might be working against us, creating an alternate reality to reduce our anxiety), the way forward will remain unclear.

Intervening. Interventions are based on hypotheses of what is understood to be happening. Interventions are experiments. Strategic planning is the best current guess to go forward. But as initiatives are set in motion to move organizations forward, one must always continue to collect data.

Arguably, Lee, on the evening of the second day of battle at Gettysburg, had an incomplete understanding of the situation he faced. There are many reasons for the incompleteness of this information—his assisting staff was too small, his cavalry was missing, two of his three principal commanders lacked experience in their new roles and were therefore unable to grasp the overarching situation they confronted, and another is Lee's own compromised beliefs about his army's abilities, to name just a few.

But for whatever reasons, Lee's hypothesis that evening was faulty. This led to a plan for the next day that would lead to disaster. Faulty interpretation will always lead to flawed intervention.

Direct intentional conversations. The leader needs to generate heat in the system (but not too much) to get the system to deal with transformational challenges. Therefore, in order to call attention to realities that may have been completely overlooked and ignored, the leader must encourage intentional conversations that permit the salient issues to emerge. Every organization with a great culture has safe places where people can speak their minds, express their dissent, and call their leaders to account. Are there places within your organization where people can speak their minds without fear of retribution?

Meade conducted an intentional conversation the evening of the second day of battle and came up not only with a workable plan going forward but also with buy-in from his commanders. Lee had no such conversation that same evening, and by taking counsel within himself, he led his troops to disaster.

Identifying the transformational issues. Hopefully, once on the balcony, the transformational leader can more easily spot the transformational issues at play—the gap between espoused values and those values used to make key decisions and the competing commitments that snarl the organization in incongruence. Once seen, the leader then presents to the stakeholders what he understands to be those transformational issues.

Arguably, Abraham Lincoln was one of the few men, both North and South, who was able to be on the balcony and clearly see the competing values that faced our nation at its critical crossroads. Everyone else at that time seemed to be "in the weeds," noting only the most obvious current struggles. As a result, Lincoln was able to place before the public the transformational issues that Americans faced. And thus, the little speech he crafted to dedicate the cemetery is still memorized and recited in schoolrooms across the nation.

Framing the issue. How an issue is framed is critical—eighty percent of the answer is in the question. Our minds insist on framing all issues and experiences in one way or another. And often those frames we manufacture are not useful to achieving the success we desire (raising healthy kids, bringing a new product into the marketplace, building a structure that is on time and below cost). How can I frame this issue so that the stakeholders can grasp the issue and move forward?

Note Lincoln's framing in his address. There were a deliberate crafting of the message in biblical language (e.g., "four score and seven") and a cadence that shaped the address as poetry more than any other medium. There is the metaphor of conception and birth. There is the idea that the nation was founded on one compelling proposition, that all men are created equal. Then there is the reframe, that the crowd was not there to dedicate that cemetery. That had already been accomplished by those who had fought and died there. The dedication was for all of us to be dedicated to the unfinished work that the soldiers who fought there had begun. And what was that unfinished work? That government of the people, by the people, for the people (not government led by an elite monarchy or dictatorship) would not perish from the earth. Democratic forms of government are by nature very fragile. The watching world assumed they could not succeed. When certain people groups within those nations felt disenfranchised, they would pull out, thus destroying that nation. So we, the living, must constantly rededicate ourselves to this unfinished work. This is what makes Lincoln's speech so compelling, even today. The work is not finished, even now. When people begin to think that the work is finished, and rest on what others have accomplished before us, we are then on very precarious ground.

Giving back the work. The work (when it is transformational) is not yours (as the leader). The work belongs to the stakeholders. They would like you to embrace the work, while they sit back and wait. But they must do the work. And so often leaders, when handed the work of others, are more than happy to dive in applying technical solutions to a problem that is not theirs to solve in the first place. As Lincoln said:

> *It is rather for us to be here dedicated to the great*
> *task remaining before us*
> *That from these honored dead we take increased*
> *devotion to that cause*
> *For which they gave the last full measure of devotion*

Managing levels of anxiety. Remember, if the stress is too low, people will feel no anxiety that moves them toward action. Therefore, the leaders must find ways to raise the anxiety. But if the stress is too high, people will become paralyzed and will be also unable to act, a situation demanding that the leader lower the anxiety so productive thinking can occur. To meet transformational challenges, people have to go through a period of painful adjustment, absorb various forms of loss, and refashion loyalties to people to whom they feel beholden.

Tolerating ambiguity. Transformational issues are fraught with ambiguity (as you hopefully have seen in the previous chapters). And that is exactly what no one wants to hear. We want to hear the leader frame a clear problem along with a clear way forward. But a complex world with competing values does not lend itself to easy answers, and ambiguity will always abound.

Providing a safe environment. If a safe environment is not provided, people will not have enough trust to enter into the transformational work they must perform. Safe environments are created by leaders who are internally aligned and therefore can be trusted. They allow the elephant in the room to emerge. They protect the voice of dissent. They are not afraid to empower those around them.

And once that safe environment has been provided, the people can have the conflict (blue zone) that is necessary to wrestle through the competing values and cobble together a way forward.

Take Action on Transformational Issues

Read through the following cases and answer the questions that follow:

Case no. 1: The CEO of a fairly large corporation began to realize that one of his employees in the senior leadership team was chronically late for work. The CEO decided that the best way to handle this was to institute a time clock. Immediately, the morale plummeted with all the other employees.

Case no. 2: You are asked to stay late to finish a project at work. You are also the coach of your child's soccer team, and there is a game tonight. You go to your supervisor and explain the situation. Your supervisor says, "I can't make this decision for you. You'll have to make the decision yourself."

Case no. 3: A supervisor has just been told that she will have to move her team—about ten people—to a different building on campus about a mile from where they are now situated. In a staff meeting, she explains to her team that they will be moving over the weekend. She further explains that the reason they are moving is because it makes more sense for them to be colocated with other elements of their organization. After she makes the announcement, the group starts complaining loudly, protesting what has happened, and "bad-mouthing" the organization and the arbitrary ways in which decisions are made.

Case no. 4: The stated policy for an organization was as follows: We expect complete devotion to your work when you are here at work. But when you are home, we expect you to be totally present to your family and leave work at work. A supervisor in team meeting stated, "This is crunch time for us. This project must be completed in two weeks, and several of you are critical to its completion, so keep your cell phones handy." Your family vacation begins in two days and is supposed to last for a week. It's been approved for months.

Answer these questions:

- What is the nature of the problem? Is it technical? Transformational? A combination?
- How did those in charge handle the situation?
- What would have been a better way to handle the situation, given how you have defined the problem?

Conclusion

In three days in the summer of 1863, the country had almost ended. In three minutes in the fall of that year, America was given a "new birth of freedom." Some initially recognized Lincoln's speech to be monumental. Most did not. Some even criticized it as trivial and embarrassing. But that three-minute speech would go down as the foundational statement of what America would become going forward. And people would actually contradict Lincoln's words. People actually would "note and long remember" what he said there in addition to "what they did" there.

But for now, on that July 4ᵗʰ morning following the battle, the population of Gettysburg, as they emerged from their basements, were traumatized. They had lived through an experience that few Americans have ever experienced, having been eyewitnesses to the most horrific battle ever fought on the continent. And because that battle had been fought in the streets, alleys, and surrounding farm fields, the landscape was devastated. It would take until the next spring for the countryside to begin to regain its luster, though it would take years for all evidence of the battle to be erased (several buildings in town still bear the pockmarks of the battle).

In virtually every city, small town, village, and hamlet throughout the land, both North and South, the names of the dead from the battle were posted in public places. And people gathered—mothers, fathers, sisters, and brothers—to scan the names to see if they too had lost a loved one in this horrific struggle that apparently had no end in sight.

This battle, this war, was fast becoming America's odyssey—that defining moment in our history upon which our unfolding narrative as a nation pivoted. To understand the American people, it is important to know of the Mayflower and Jamestown, the Boston Massacre, Fort McHenry, the Constitutional Convention, and the numerous men and women who forged our nation out of the wilderness. It's important to note the wars and internal struggles that have been fought, of the push westward, and what that meant to our people and the native peoples we found already there. But none of this will gain its proper place and significance until the Civil War is grasped and understood.

And that is why the setting of the Civil War, and its most momentous battle—Gettysburg—has been, to my way of thinking, the proper backdrop to understand the nature of leadership.

Take Action

An article in *Harvard Business Review* details ten of the most important leadership competencies that were reported by leaders around the world.[33] Take a look at each of these competencies. In the first column to the right, rank yourself on a scale of 1 (low) to 5 (high) as to how well you measure up to that competency. In the second column, rank that competency as to how important you understand this competency to be (A = very high priority, B = less of a priority, C = low priority). What would add to the helpfulness of this would be to let several of your peers and subordinates rate you on these criteria.

Competency	Priority	Score
Has high ethical and moral standards thus creating a safe and trusting environment	A, B, C	1 to 5
Provides goals and objectives while allowing employees to organize their own time and work		
Clearly communicates expectations		
Has the flexibility to change opinions		
Is committed to subordinates' ongoing training		

[33] Sunnie Giles. "The most important leadership competencies, according to leaders around the world." *Harvard Business Review.* March 15, 2016

Communicates often and openly		
Is open to new ideas and approaches while fostering organizational learning		
Creates a feeling of succeeding and failing together		
Helps me grow into a next-generation leader		
Provides safety for trial and error		

About the Author

James P. Osterhaus (PhD, American University) is a senior partner with TAG. He is a dynamic executive coach and public speaker with extensive experience in helping individuals move through change, conflict, and reorganization. He brings a depth of understanding of systems and relational network thinking to his work developed from years practicing as a highly respected psychologist in Northern Virginia  in addition to consulting. Recently he has developed a Gettysburg Leadership Experience, taking teams to the battlefield discussing leadership principles. He has worked extensively with the FAA, coaching vice presidents and managers and leading workshops and seminars on various aspects of leadership. He has been quoted in the *New York Times, Los Angeles Times, Seattle Times*, and many other leading publications.

He has facilitated groups and taught seminars in numerous settings including the University of San Francisco and American University. He has also taught graduate level classes on four continents on various subjects ranging from organizational systems to communication and conflict management. Jim has authored fourteen books and written articles for magazines and trade journals around the country. His latest book, *Red Zone, Blue Zone*, details the benefits of mission-focused conflict. He has written a novel on the Civil War: *Antietam: A Harvest of Blood*.